IN PRAISE

Sacred Truths – The Backside of the Mountain
Third in the Catherine DeLong Series
Also by Linda Kendall McLendon
Unintended Lies – first in the series
& *Accidental Lives* – second in the series

Linda Kendall McLendon's debut novel **Unintended Lies** is a wonderfully catching tale that gives the reader an impression that a much more seasoned writer penned the manuscript. Her ability to assume the persona of each character, changing effortlessly from Catherine DeLong to Zane Wheeler and many other characters as she writes this novel leaves me awed. Linda manages to flow from **Unintended Lies** to her follow-up book, **Accidental Lives,** without losing the pace. The story picks up right where it left off but with more insight into the lives of the character's past, adding depth and color to each person written about. The tale will leave you with many 'aha' moments and a few 'I didn't see that coming' thoughts. Both of Linda's books are page turners which will leave the reader wanting more and waiting for the next tale to be told. They are a must read from a new author with an old soul.
Richard D. Rowland, Author of Unspoken Messages

I loved **Unintended Lies** and couldn't wait for the second one! The book is so easy to read and to get hooked on immediately. I loved all of her characters and how she wove the tale around them and their unintended lies. Each page had me wondering what would happen next and how would the book end? Once it did end, I wanted the next book right away so I could continue to be a fly on the wall in the character's lives. A terrific tale of love, comedy and suspense. Couldn't wait for book two, **Accidental Lives.** Part 2 kept me going. I almost feel addicted to her characters. I loved the first book and couldn't wait for the second book. Now she has done it again, keeping me intrigued in the story even more than before and now I can't wait for the third book to come out! What a great storyteller...even a story within the story. Please finish book 3 soon so I can find out the end of the story. Great job!

Leslie Corcoran

A charming, nail-biting suspense, **Unintended Lies,** will sweep you off your feet and leave you breathless craving more. I received a complimentary paperback copy in exchange for review, and my heart was just racing through the suspenseful developing mysteries and newly budding romance. Any horse or dog lover and contemporary romance/suspense reader will surely fall for these charming and wholesome down to earth written characters. I loved the secrets that were slowly unveiled, and kept me guessing even after the pages ceased turning. I would highly recommend!

Missy

Accidental Lives is the second in the series featuring Catherine DeLong. This volume brings everyone together and firmly establishes all of the coincidental and not so coincidental connections and ties of husbands, wives, lovers, mothers, fathers, and the way we never really get over our growing up pains. There is enough drama, self-doubt and emotion to satisfy any angst-ridden teenager, but her characters are drawn so real you end up living with them as they try and carry on, ordinary people caught in a series of extraordinary circumstances. They are so real, in fact, that at times you want to go, knock on the door, and tell them to stop the nonsense, tell each other the truth, and get on with it! McLendon draws a beautiful picture of the land they live on, and adds color with her Native American history as an element of the characters. An excellent addition to the "chick lit" genre. Looking forward to the third volume when they do "get it all together!"

Anonymous

Accidental Lives is the gripping follow-up novel to Linda Kendall McLendon's *Unintended Lies* about Catherine DeLong, who leaves her old life after the loss of her husband in a car accident and moves to a ranch in northern Florida. Recently retired agents, Zane and Buck, lure her into haunting questions about her husband's past while she tries to move on with her life.

Zane has his own past to sort out. He has been away from home for decades and feels the urgent need to visit his aging mother and his old friend Parker, who works on his parents' ranch and was more of a father to him than his own.

Readers will have a lot of surprises in this book, and so will Catherine. I found Accidental Lives to read in a fast-paced manner, and never once did my attention lag. It's the kind of book you read in a day because you can't put it down, and then you wish it hadn't ended. Fortunately, McLendon plans to write one final book in this series. Good news for me because I've grown to love these characters who have their quirks and issues, but are good people who care about one another and are trying just to find a little happiness and make sense of their pasts. I was shocked in all the appropriate places by the surprises that happened in the book, and I read on, waiting for the stunning climactic scene to see how Catherine would react when she found out about the big secret that had been kept from her.

I know readers who loved "Unintended Lies" will be anxious to read "Accidental Lives," and they will be impatient for the final book where all the various plot strands will finally be woven together. To keep the reader's interest over three volumes is no easy task, but so far, McLendon has done it deftly, subtly, yet powerfully, always leaving us wanting more. Her readers come to feel like they really know all the characters in this book, and they cheer for Catherine, Zane, and all the good characters, sometimes even just wanting to give one of them a hug. I can't wait for the final book.

Tyler R. Tichelaar

SACRED TRUTHS

The Backside of the Mountain

Third in the
Catherine DeLong Series

Linda Kendall
McLendon

Sacred Truths
The Back Side of the Mountain
by Linda Kendall McLendon

Copyright © January 2022 Linda Kendall McLendon
ALL RIGHTS RESERVED

This is a work of fiction. Names, characters, places and incidents either are products of the author's imagination or are used fictitiously. Any resemblance to actual events or locales or persons, living or dead, is entirely coincidental.

EXCEPT FOR BRIEF TEXT QUOTED AND APPROPRIATELY CITED IN OTHER WORKS, NO PART OF THIS BOOK MAY BE REPRODUCED IN ANY FORM, BY PHOTOCOPYING OR BY ELECTRONIC OR MECHANICAL MEANS, INCLUDING INFORMATION-STORAGE-OR-RETRIEVAL SYSTEMS, WITHOUT PERMISSION IN WRITING FROM THE COPYRIGHT OWNER/AUTHOR.

ISBN-13: 978-0-9909040-9-0

ACKNOWLEDGMENTS

There have been so many special people in my life that it would be unfair to try to name them. You have inspired me, loved me, encouraged me, or made me furious. Let me just say, if you are still on the planet, then you know who you are and how you influenced me. If you are not, then you know who you are, because I am constantly pestering you from the down side of heaven.

For all who have come full circle
in and out of my life,
You have either been my teacher or my student.

For those who have been my teachers,
I hope the ripples you started in me will continue to move through those who have come after your lessons.

For all who have traveled with me
on this writing adventure, especially my fellow writers
In our Word Weavers Group, who critiqued my work
and inspired me by theirs,
Without you, there would be no reason for me to write, or
the readers to read.
Thank you!

I especially want to dedicate this trilogy to my dear friend, Catherine Dowling, whose life was tragically ended too soon too many years ago by a drunk driver. You have lived in my heart always. My life would not have been the same without your spontaneous, crazy entry and untimely, devastating departure. I recall you saying, "Girl, you can do anything." I certainly have striven to make that so, including writing these three novels. I know you are proud of everything I've accomplished, but I couldn't have done it without you, my guardian angel and guide. I owe a huge thank you to your parents, Lee and Ham, and your brother, Jim, who took over for you as my favorite cheerleaders. They continue the hurrahs and attagirls!!

Thank you to William Greenleaf, author and owner of Greenleaf Literary Services and Tyler Tichelaar, PhD and award-winning author. Your critiques and edits have made me a better writer than I ever dreamed I could be. I look forward to collaborating more and continuing to be in awe of your many talents.

I AM GRATEFUL!

In Loving Memory of LELAND GROUND
Blackfeet Nation
We became better human beings by knowing him.
Mind, body and spirit

CHAPTER 1

"Go inside and listen to your body, because your body will never lie to you. Your mind will play tricks, but the way you feel in your heart, in your guts, is the truth."

~ Miguel Ruiz

The one thing Catherine DeLong knew for sure was that James didn't know about the beach house, so she would feel relatively safe there. She pulled into the last gas station before the Alachua/High Springs I-75 entrance ramps. The automatic shutoff clicked. She sucked in a deep breath, waited to retrieve the receipt, and got into her car. Parking abruptly at the end of the paved area, she took a moment to contemplate her decision. Pulling north toward Jacksonville would mean boarding a plane headed to Montana and Zane. Turning south, she wasn't sure of the outcome. The clock was ticking and so was her window of opportunity. She picked up her cellphone. It was a relief to hear a familiar voice.

"Hamilton, it's Catherine. Sorry for calling so early, but I have a question."

Her stepfather cleared his throat and said, "Oh, honey, I have been worried about you. It's been way too long."

"I know. A lot has happened. I need your help."

"What is it?"

"I was wondering if the house on the beach is available. Do you still even own it? I mean, I would rent it from you. I need to get away for a bit."

She hadn't spent a minute preparing for this conversation. She was going on what her gut was telling her, while fighting what was tugging at her heart. She swallowed hard, waiting.

"The house is vacant. I was going to have it painted, but that can wait. When are you coming? And I won't hear of you paying."

The sound of Hamilton's voice steadied her. He had always been consistent, thoughtful, caring.

"I'll arrive today. I'm packed and in my car. I'll explain later when I see you."

"Honey, you don't have to explain a thing to me. If you don't mind a few smudges on the walls, it won't be a problem. I was going to get it ready for the winter season, but I'll still have time. I'll leave the keys at the front desk at my office, but I'd love to give you a hug."

"Sounds good. And there's another thing—would you mind not saying anything to Mom right away or Kiki. I need a little time to myself."

She knew he wouldn't question her. When she had left home, landed her first job, and married James, he had trusted her. Hamilton had been the one person who supported her decisions, even if they sometimes turned out wrong.

"Catherine, whatever you want, it's fine. Promise me you will keep me informed. I want to know you're okay."

"Of course, I will, and I appreciate this very much. It's nothing really, so don't worry."

"Let me know if you need anything."

"Okay. Well, I'm going to get on the road. I think it will take me maybe five hours. I'll see you soon."

"Love you. Stay safe."

"I will. Bye, and thank you."

Next, she would have to make the tough phone call, but it was only nine o'clock in the morning. Too early to call Montana.

She'd have to wait to tell Zane due to the time difference. She would do it when she stopped to fill the gas tank again. She felt relieved and somewhat scared.

Turning the car onto the road in front of the gas station, she accelerated onto the entrance ramp and headed south toward Jensen Beach. She needed time to process what the hell had happened to her life. With the exception of her stepfather, she felt betrayed by every male she had allowed her heart to care about. Now, she wasn't even sure what to feel toward Zane. He had kept his secrets from her too.

The heavy feeling in the front of her forehead preceding a headache was coming on, making her realize she'd been holding her breath most of the time she was talking to Hamilton. The tightness in her chest made her feel like something was about to happen, but she had no way of knowing what it was. She had to let it go, put it all out of her mind, and focus on driving to avoid being a casualty, but then that would be an answer, wouldn't it?

"Stop it. Stop it right now. You know you don't want to go there," she said out loud. "It's okay to take some time. Breathe." It was going to be a long drive.

~~~~~

Zane Wheeler heard a rooster crow, stretched, and got out of bed. It was going to be a slow day at the ranch while waiting until it was time to pick up Catherine at the airport. She wouldn't arrive until late afternoon. It had been too many days since he had held her in his arms. He felt elated about sharing her with his mother. He also couldn't wait for Catherine to meet Parker Iron Crow and then, when they were alone, he would tell her what he had recently learned. It would be good to have her at his childhood home and to reveal everything to her.

When his mother told him her secrets, it had been a shock to Zane, and yet deep inside, he had always known something wasn't quite right with all the goings on at the ranch. It was a relief to finally put all the pieces into place. Now, he would be including the woman he wanted to spend the rest of his life with. He could hardly wait to see her.

Silently making his way down the stairs, Zane stepped out onto the front porch into the semi-darkness and sat on one of the rocking chairs. Soon the ranch would be abuzz with the normal morning routine. He would have to fight his impatience, while waiting out the hours before time to leave. He was glad Catherine was coming in summer when the weather was more predictable.

It wasn't long before his mother, Maggie White Calf, slipped out the front door and sat next to him. She was still in her nightgown, with a soft, long red robe wrapped around her. She had low deerskin moccasins on her feet. Slowly rocking back and forth, Zane and Maggie enjoyed the quiet of the morning. The sun began to send its soft pink rays toward the mountains.

"Anxious for this day to come?" she asked.

"Yes, you know I am. I sure hope all goes well with her flights."

"Watched the weather last night; it should be a perfect Montana day for her."

"I'm sure she's worried about leaving her animals again."

"The Matthews will do fine with them."

"I know that, and you know that, but Catherine doesn't know them like we do."

"As soon as she sees you, she'll forget all about them."

Zane smiled. "I doubt it, but it is a nice thought. I hope she doesn't get cold feet."

"Stop worrying. She said she would come."

"Yes, she did, but it is still going to be a long day waiting."

One of the rocking chairs squeaked as they slowly continued to rock. Silently looking out across the vast flatlands toward the mountains, Zane reached over and squeezed his mother's hand.

Scared Truths

"Thanks for spending some quiet time with me this morning."

~~~~~

Catherine had been driving for what felt like hours. She had fallen into the monotonous rhythm of setting the cruise control and staying out of the way of inconsiderate drivers. The Okahumpka Plaza, her proclaimed Pit Stop, was coming up soon. She needed to stretch her legs. It would do her good to move around and grab some caffeine. She would also make the dreaded call to Zane. A sign suddenly revealed it was only two miles to the plaza.

After topping off the gas tank, she spent some time in the restroom, washed her face, then picked up a soda and small bag of chips in the convenience store. She slid back in the car, moved to a parking slot and munched on a few chips. Now she had to call Zane and tell him she wasn't coming. She dreaded it, plus she wasn't completely happy about her last-minute decision. If she had thought about it, she would have gone back to the house to grab Friskie, his crate, and all his goodies. He could have kept her company at the beach house. He had been so fragile when she rescued him from Buck's feed store. Poor tiny black fuzzball. She could kick herself.

Washing down the last of the chips, she grabbed her cellphone from the console. It took a few seconds to look up the phone number for Zane's mother and push the button. The phone rang three, four times, and then he answered.

"Zane, is that you?"

"Hey, Catherine. Where are you?"

She took a deep breath and felt the familiar pang in her stomach.

"I'm going to go ahead and say it. I'm not coming."

She waited through a long silence.

"Okay," he finally said. "What happened? Tell me you're okay?" His voice sounded worried.

"Nothing happened. It's me. I need some time. I was all packed and ready to head to the airport and I got to the interstate and I couldn't do it. I'm sorry."

There was dead silence for a while before he spoke.

"Catherine, I knew I should have come there when that jerk showed up."

"It's okay, Zane. I need to sort things out. I have a place to go James doesn't know about. I'll be fine."

"I'm not sure I like this. I think you would be safer here in Montana with me."

Catherine sighed.

"I'm going to be fine, but I wish I had gone back and picked up Friskie and his things. I'm worried about him adjusting again."

More silence, and then Zane said, "I think he'll be okay. The Matthews will spoil him. I'm worried about you, though. Can I do something, say something, anything to change your mind? Can I come there? Where are you? I'll come get you."

"No, not now. I need to be away for a while. You won't be able to reach me. I know you need to decide about things, too. I'll call you."

"Catherine, are you sure this is what you want to do?"

"I'm not sure about anything. It's what I'm doing for right now."

"You do know I love you, don't you? This doesn't have anything to do with that does it?" Zane asked.

She could hear the tension in his voice.

"I'm not sure how I feel about love right now. James said he loved me. I have so many different feelings, ideas in my mind about the word."

"All I know is how I feel, and I don't want to spend another minute without you."

"I'm sure you mean it, but I don't know how to feel right now. I have to go. I'll be in touch soon. I'm sorry."

As she pushed the button cutting him off, a flood of tears streamed down her face. She hadn't wanted to have this conversation. Nothing had felt right since James' stupid fake death—not since she had been forced to create a new life, and not since she and Zane had accidentally found each other. Now there were even more questions. She wiped her tears, blew her nose and slowly drove through the parking lot heading south into who knew what.

Catherine was relieved when she finally exited the turnpike and headed east. She stopped at Hamilton's office on Ricco Terrace and picked up the keys. The receptionist said her stepfather had walked across the street to the bank. She asked for the address of the beach house, and dashed out to her car. Even though a hug would have felt wonderful, not having to explain anything to Hamilton was a blessing.

She turned north on Indian River Drive, took the causeway across toward the ocean, and headed north on A1A. The house was on the beach side about a mile north. She unloaded her few pieces of luggage, her cosmetic bag, and her laptop, and dropped onto the couch. She was so tired she didn't even take off her shoes. She simply pulled one of the throw pillows up under her neck and drifted off to sleep.

~~~~~

CHAPTER 2

Her family's two-story had a beautiful view of the sand dunes and the ocean. Catherine's thoughts drifted back to when she had spent long lost days at the beach. The house wasn't far from the pavilions and bulkhead where she and her cousins, Waylon and Justin, and her sister, Kiki, had played as small children. She had been drawn to walk down there and sit on a bench staring out across the sea. She could almost hear their haunting laughter, the sounds of them splashing in the water, rushing to catch sand fleas, throw crabs up on the shore, or scurrying through the hot sand to get something to eat at the Sandpiper.

Her Aunt Josie, the boys' mother, along with the lifeguard, Tony Latuso, had kept a watchful eye on them. Even as a little girl, she knew Tony was handsome, tan with jet black hair, Italian, with the biggest heart in the world. On rainy days, he would paint the girls' toenails, teach them card games, wrap them in big soft towels if they got chilled, or let them hang out inside the lifeguard's shed. It was up underneath the pavilion and kept them out of the wind, rain, or the pelting wind-driven sand.

Back then, her mother, Elizabeth, worked at the Sandpiper at the counter serving customers. Catherine had loved the old place. The wooden floors would get gritty from the sand falling off the people's feet. She loved how it smelled of fried onions, burgers, and hot dogs and the murmur of the voices when she opened the screen door and walked inside. The place was completely built of knotty pine harvested out on the Martin Grade. Even the ceiling was made of the same wood with beautiful thick beams. The hotter it got, the better the place smelled.

A jukebox was in the back. Her mother would slip her a coin and away she would go to push her favorite buttons and play a song. She loved the way it was lit up and watching the arm grab a forty-five vinyl record, placing it gently on the turnstile.

Fishing nets draped from the ceilings had items tucked up in them people had found on the beach. There were dried starfish, puffer fish, an occasional conch or cowry. Her favorite was a big green glass float they said had come off of a Japanese fishing boat. She tried to imagine the trip the float must have taken to land on the beach there. Back then, it conjured up all sorts of ideas for her about the ship and the fish the crew must have caught. She couldn't help but wonder if that was all they had been doing. Had they been spying?

Catherine didn't know how long she sat lost in her childhood memories. She knew her reclusive behavior wasn't good for her. Other than going out to buy food, she hadn't done anything except walk the beach and think. She had called Mrs. Matthews, Buck's mother, to check on her animals. Effie had sounded surprised when she told her she wasn't in Montana with Zane. Catherine asked her not to say anything to anyone.

~~~~~

After a week of no contact with Catherine, Zane was ready to leave and find her. He couldn't go back to her ranch since Buck's parents, Roan and Effie Matthews, were staying there caring for Catherine's animals, as well as his horse, Trouble. He could have barged in on them, stayed in the guest bedroom, but it wasn't right. After all, it wasn't his home.

He had called Roan and knew he had been working the horses. It seemed like everyone was doing fine, except for Friskie, who had been a little hard to win over this time until

Zane reminded Roan about his love of bacon. It had done the trick.

Zane banged his hat on his knee to get the dust off before he made his way up the back steps and into the kitchen. His mother was busy at the sink paring potatoes. He leaned in and kissed her on the cheek.

"That makes me giggle. It's like I have my little boy back."

"Well, I'm not so little and I won't be if you don't quit feeding me so much."

He pulled out a chair and sat at the head of the table as she dried her hands on her apron and joined him.

"What is it?" she asked.

"Mother, I don't know what to do. I thought she'd have called by now. I hate to leave you, but I think I'm going to try and find her."

Zane grabbed her hands as she stretched them out in front of her across the table. They sat for a few moments looking into each other's eyes.

"I'm not ready to let you go. I finally got you back."

"I know, but I'm afraid if I don't go, too much time will pass and something will happen or not happen."

"Maybe you should wait."

"I don't want to wait. I want an answer. I want to know she's okay."

The way his mother curled a wisp of hair behind her ear reminded him of other days.

"Zane, you would have heard if something had happened. Buck would let you know. Have you talked to him?" She slid her hand back in his.

Zane hadn't talked to anyone since a few days ago when he called Buck. He hadn't mentioned Catherine wasn't with him and Buck hadn't said anything about it either. He was heartsick about not hearing from her. He was happy to be home with his mother and Iron Crow, but nothing made him feel okay about Catherine's decision.

"No, I haven't talked to Buck in a few days. He didn't say anything except Catherine had checked in with his mother about her animals. That's all he said. I don't think he knows she's not here."

"I see. Then she must be okay."

"I'm sure she's okay, but I'm not sure about us. I'm certain she feels betrayed by me."

"Give her a bit of time, Zane. Wait. I'm feeling like you will hear from her soon."

"Have you been into the tea leaves again?" Zane smiled.

"No. I can feel it in my bones."

"Well, I hope your bones are reading this one right, Mom, 'cause I'm not so sure."

~~~~~

Falling back into the ranch routine had been easy, but emotionally, it had changed the moment Zane's mother and Parker Iron Crow revealed the secrets they had kept. It was no wonder his purported father, Foster Thomas Wheeler, had been so angry all the time. Surely Foster knew from the beginning Iron Crow wasn't just a hired hand? Had he put up with it to save face, or was he a bigger man than any of them had realized? It was something Zane had to ponder.

Riding out on the range gave him peaceful time to think. It had been many years since he and Buck had taken off and created their illustrious careers with the National Security Agency. It had been a wild and crazy ride at times, but they couldn't deny what they had accomplished for their country. The entire training facility was dedicated in their honor. They had come from the dirt of the earth, the soul of Montana, and accomplished much more than either of them could have imagined.

The United States Intelligence Community had become their new family and expanded their horizons. Zane had found an entire new world beyond the ranch. Ironic now, when things should be settling down for him back at home, Catherine was tugging at his heart, causing him to want to leave again.

He squeezed his horse into a lope and caught up with Iron Crow. He needed to make some decisions, and there was one person who could certainly guide him on the journey.

CHAPTER 3

The phone rang three times before Celia Fenmore answered. Catherine was relieved to hear her half-sister's voice. She had barely wrapped her mind around the fact they were related, and so she felt apprehensive about having another conversation with her.

"Hi, Celia. It's Catherine. How are you? Am I bothering you?"

"Oh, not at all, Catherine. I'm glad to hear from you."

"I'm in town, staying on the beach. I wondered if we could get together."

"I have Olivia home full time since school is out for the summer. Would you mind if she joined us? I mean, if you do, I'm sure my grandmother wouldn't mind spending time with her. When did you want to get together? Today?"

"Oh, it doesn't have to be today." Catherine was scrambling. She hadn't expected Celia to be available so soon.

"I have some things I'd like to drop off at my grandmothers anyway. In fact, I'll leave Olivia there. It will be easier. I can call you back in a few minutes and let you know for sure."

They said quick goodbyes and Catherine waited, impatiently drumming her fingers on the kitchen counter. She stared out the sliding doors at the turquoise sea. She shouldn't even be in Jensen Beach, let alone stirring things up by contacting Celia. She jumped when her cellphone rang. Celia would come to the beach house within the hour alone.

Catherine shook her head. *What are you getting yourself into?*

In what seemed like no time, she heard a soft knock at the door, and as soon as she opened it, without any words, the sisters embraced. Catherine invited Celia to sit outside on the patio. The soft breeze blew over the sand dunes as the waves gently played their methodical sounds. It was mid-afternoon, and only a few people were walking along the shoreline.

"So," Celia asked, "what brought you back to Jensen?"

"Oh, I guess you could say I needed a change of scenery," Catherine lied.

"Well, you certainly picked a beautiful setting. This is a nice house. You do know it was the first home built on Hutchinson Island? That is, besides the House of Refuge, as far as domestic houses. There may have been native homes of sorts before Hutchinson's plantation was built in the early 1800s."

"No, I didn't think about it. It's hard to believe this island was inhabited that long ago. This house belongs to my stepfather and mother."

"It was originally built by the same three men who owned the Sandpiper, the little hamburger joint, and the old hotel. They didn't like living where they worked, so they built this house."

"My mother worked at the restaurant, the Sandpiper, I mean," Catherine said. "The men who owned it were her bosses. Small world, isn't it?"

"Yes, it is. They raised a bit of controversy back then when some of the old timers didn't like the idea of buildings on the beach. They'd die if they saw the development on the island now."

"I never thought about it until recently, you know, when I came back to take care of Uncle Walton. I was shocked to see the nuclear plant perched out here on a barrier reef. It scared me. But as far as those men go, my remembrance of them were the little things they did for me. They brought my sister, Kiki, and me dolls from England. I still have mine."

"The doll must have meant a lot to you."

"It wasn't only about the dolls. They were kind to us. They had come into our lives at a time when our family was falling apart. They were hugely supportive of my mother."

"I'm sorry."

"Oh, no, don't be. After all, if that hadn't happened, you and I wouldn't be having this conversation. You probably wouldn't have existed if my parents hadn't split up."

"That's an interesting and nice way of looking at it." Celia smiled.

"I guess it is. I'm finding interesting ways of looking at a lot of things these days."

Catherine's voice drifted off as she realized she was moving into troubling thoughts and caught herself. She didn't know exactly how much to share; after all, it hadn't been long since she had discovered she and Celia were half-sisters. If her father hadn't met Celia's mother? If her parents had still been together? There were lots of what ifs.

"Would you like something to drink? I'll be right back." Catherine didn't even wait for Celia to respond. She brought back a small tray with two glasses of iced tea, crackers, and cheese. She asked Celia what her family was doing over the summer.

"Olivia is quite active with anything to do with water or nature. She loves attending workshops at the children's museum. They have a great program at the oceanographic group here, and she loves the activities at Barley Barber Swamp. There is an almost endless number of things to do."

"That's wonderful. When I was a kid, we spent all our time roaming through the swamp, the woods, or at this beach."

"She's not too far from that, except it's supervised, and the flora and fauna are most likely a lot more civilized than when you were younger. I bet you could tell some tales."

"Oh, yes. It's a wonder we survived as well as we did."

Catherine remembered the day her cousin, Waylon, had protected them all by killing a small ground rattler with a piece of a stump he'd suddenly grabbed. It had struck the heel of one of their friend's shoes below his ankle. She shuddered and then looked up.

"Oh, Celia, I'm sorry. I got lost in a memory of a moment long ago in the woods."

~~~~~

Catherine and Celia weren't together long before they decided to take a walk on the beach. Catherine kicked at shells and hurled a few stones into the waves as they walked north along the shoreline. Maybe it was the steady rhythm of the sea, the soft ocean breezes swirling her hair around her face, or the salt spray occasionally misting her body, but she began to relax for the first time in what seemed like a long time. She let her shoulders droop, her arms swing, and felt the sand beneath her feet.

"I've hit a rough spot, Celia, and I don't know what to do. I ran away from home, and now I don't know where I go from here."

"That's tough. So, tell me, what are your options?"

"Do you have a while?" Catherine chuckled.

Celia pulled her cellphone from her pocket, checked the time, and said, "I have about an hour. Will that do?"

Catherine let out a big sigh and began. "I was married to James quite a while and, in a nutshell, he turned out to be much different than I thought. First, they told me he had been killed in a car accident. Then, I was told he was mixed up with the government and had been murdered. The car had caught on fire. There was the condition of his body, the funeral. It was horrible and I was devastated. It got even worse when I discovered he was really alive, but had been in protective custody, and given a new identity."

"Wait a minute. You mean he wasn't dead at all?"

"It was crazy. I went back over every little detail of our relationship and my life with him, trying to figure out when the deceit began and how I missed it."

"It must have been difficult. But you can't blame yourself, you know."

"It was quite a roller-coaster ride, and for what? After I had been grieving, started a new life with someone else, James suddenly shows up and wants to explain it all. He had surgery to alter his appearance, so I didn't even recognize him. I was extremely angry at him, the lies, and shocked at how he looked. I barely even know what I said to him. Who was he? It was brutal. I couldn't believe what he'd put me through."

"It must have really surprised and hurt you."

"I thought I had gotten through it, but I don't think you ever get over the death of someone you love. I wasn't even used to him not being in my life. You know I moved to North Florida and the farm. I was getting settled and then my uncle became ill. I came down here and it seemed like my uncle was gone so quickly. First, it was James, and then it was Uncle Walton. The grief was overwhelming."

"I know it was a lot. I remember how fragile you were when I met you."

"I find it interesting you saw me as fragile. I believed I was strong. I felt tough—tough until I went home and fell apart. I wasn't there a few minutes before I collapsed. The doctor said it was a virus and exhaustion. I was out for almost two weeks."

"I had no idea. I'm sorry you went through that."

"Well, it had a happy side for a while. This will sound ridiculous, but I had hired a man to care for my ranch and the animals. He was living there while I was here. He's the one who took care of me when I was ill. He found a doctor to come to the house, and he literally nursed me back to health."

"He's impressive."

Catherine picked up a large flat sandstone about the size of a saucer and flung it sideways across a wave. She watched it skip twice and then disappear into the white foam at the top of the next wave.

"Impressive? Yes, that's a good word for Zane. He was quite impressive. We had talked on the phone while I was at

Uncle Walton's. Then while I was recovering, I asked him to stay on longer, until I got my strength back. I hadn't intended for him to be anything but a hired hand, but then . . . ."

"Oh, I think I'm beginning to see where this is heading." Celia giggled softly.

"I seriously don't know how it happened, but we had a lot in common, and he was so amazing with the horses and the dogs. I met him because I rescued his horse, Trouble, when his truck broke down. It's a long story."

Celia laughed and looked at her phone again. "Another twenty minutes before I have to go."

"Well, let's turn around so we end up back at the house in the nick of time."

Celia picked up a cockleshell and slid it into her pocket. "My grandmother loves these."

"How is she?" Catherine asked.

"Not so well. I'll tell you about it next time we talk, but for now you better tell me the rest of this story."

"I know how crazy this is going to sound, so brace yourself. It turned out Zane worked for the government, and so did his friend—the guy who runs the feed store in the town where I live—both of them knew all about my husband's situation. Zane kept information from me about James he says was to protect me. So, these two men, Zane Wheeler and Buck Matthews, were all mixed up in my life."

"Okay, so there were three men deceiving you? Right? How awful."

"And then, even though it was planned, Zane went off to Montana to see his mother, and I was left alone on the ranch. That's when James called pretending to be a reporter from the local newspaper wanting to interview me about reinventing my life. Said something about newcomers to the area. I was so gullible. I fell for it. I was fooled once again. He scared me, and at the same time, made me furious."

"How awful."

"It was unnerving. I was supposed to join Zane in Montana, but all this made me start doubting my relationship with him too. I didn't know who to believe, so instead of going to Zane, I freaked out and fled here."

"Wow! I can see why you are bewildered right now."

"Yes, and I only touched the tip of the iceberg."

They walked up the dunes and onto the patio behind the house.

"Well, I hate to do this to you," Celia said, "but I promised I wouldn't be away long. Mimi has been having some memory issues and I worry. We will get together again soon. I promise. Call me. After eight is fine. Olivia's in bed."

They walked around the house to Celia's car and embraced.

"I'll be okay."

"I'm sure you will. I mean it, though. Call me if you need me. We can at least chat on the phone." They hugged, and Catherine waited until Celia drove away. It was comforting because, for the first time in a long time, she had a woman to confide in.

CHAPTER 4

The summer was fleeting, and there were chores to do before the aspen leaves turned yellow and began to fall. Maggie White Calf busied herself in the garden pulling out the few remaining potatoes and onions. She would put them in the root cellar. It had been one of the things she asked Foster for when she moved into his house. He had the men dig it out for her so she could go into it from inside the cellar in winter or through heavy doors outside from the garden during summer. The house sat on a knoll, making the cellar easy to construct.

As she worked the rich soil, Maggie was feeling the pressure of seeing Zane in such a state. She could tell by his face and body language he was in turmoil. All her instincts told her he was going to leave soon to try to find Catherine. Her heart was aching with wanting him to linger with them a little longer. There were too many things she still needed to say to him, and she was certain Iron Crow wouldn't want him to leave so soon either.

The old screen door slammed behind her as she struggled with the bounty in her apron. She placed her morning harvest in a basket along with jars of vegetables she had recently canned so she could take them the next time she went down to the cellar. It had taken a bit of experimenting to figure out which vegetables stored best next to each other. She discovered certain ones emitted gases and caused the others to rot. Things like cabbage and onions had their own odors, which tainted their neighbors. She learned to store some of them in sawdust from the mill or loose clean soil to remedy the problem. It had been a labor of love to feed her family and all the men who worked on the ranch.

Maggie was grateful their son had come home and she and Iron Crow had finally told him the truth. They had carried their secrets far too long. She had always suspected Zane knew something was wrong between Foster and her. She had played the role of Foster's wife all those years so he could hold his place in the community. He didn't want anyone thinking he was anything less than the cattle baron he portrayed. Foster possessed great power and influence through the operation of his large ranch and his herds of beef cattle and horses. He had proved his manhood by producing a son to take on his Western heritage. How many times had she heard him say, "This territory would have been nothing without my family and what they did for it. None of this would have happened without them. We are the Wheelers, for God's sake, descended from a line of wheelwrights—the people who made and repaired wheels—the wheels that significantly altered the course of the Wild Wild West." It was the same rant every time. Maybe if he said it often enough, he could believe it.

Maggie had taken the brunt of Foster's rage when he discovered Zane had fled with Buck Matthews. He blamed her, accused her of knowing all along what the boys had been up to. She swore she knew nothing about it. He had thrown her across the room and was about to come at her again when Parker walked into the kitchen. She remembered it like it was yesterday. The two men had stood there staring into each other's eyes for what seemed like an eternity. All Parker said was "She didn't know. Neither did I," and Foster had turned and walked straight through the house, out the front door and climbed into his truck. Several days passed before he came back to the ranch. He never said another word to Maggie about Zane until he became ill. Funny how dying brings people to terms with living.

She shook her head and walked out on the back porch. It always brought her peace to stand and look at the mountains.

It hadn't been an easy life, but she wasn't sure she would have changed it. She had brought a wonderful boy into this world who had turned into a remarkable man. Foster had given them an opportunity no one in her family could have imagined. Getting off the reservation had been a blessing. And then there was Parker. Their love had endured through it all and now they were all together at last. She didn't want to let that go. Not yet.

~~~~

Zane waited until all the men left the kitchen and Parker had disappeared out the back door. Alone with his mother, he watched as she cleared the dishes from the old worn wooden table. How many times had they sat there with Foster, hoping they could get through dinner without an upheaval? It seemed like that man was always angry—looking for something to be enraged about. It didn't matter if it was one of the men, the cattle, or what Zane had failed to do. He would bring it up at dinner as soon as the men had left. He would go on and on about whatever it was. He and his mother would sit looking at their plates, trying not to react to his onslaught. Sometimes it worked, sometimes it didn't. Zane inhaled deeply as he shook his head, attempting to stop those memories.

"I don't know how you did it all those years, Mom."

"What are you talking about Zane? I loved living here on the ranch and cooking for the men and my family."

"That's not what I'm talking about. I'm talking about living with him."

Zane couldn't bring himself to call him anything. It was, in some ways, a huge relief not to have to call him his father. He never understood how a father could treat his son the way he had treated him, but now that he knew the truth, it made sense. Foster Wheeler had been a man running from what he considered his failure, and he had been taking it out on the people closest to him—as if they had been responsible for it.

"It wasn't all bad, Zane. He was outside most of the day working on the ranch. There were times when he was angry or upset, but mostly at night, he was bone-tired. He put up a false front for the hired hands and us, but he wasn't as strong as he appeared. You know, he didn't have anyone but us. His parents and his sister were all gone before I married him. He was at a friend's house the night their house caught on fire. He felt like he failed them. He carried a lot of demons."

"I didn't know."

"I know. We never discussed it because it was a deep wound with no cure." She wiped her hands on a small white towel and came over and sat next to Zane at the table.

"There were a lot of things you didn't know about him. He had moments when he let his guard down, but they were few and far between. Mostly, he kept it to himself."

"It's hard to wrap my head around all this. You never wanted other children? A relationship with Iron Crow?"

"Foster wanted a son. When you were born, you were enough for him. He wanted you and didn't want you all at the same time. Maybe it would be fairer to say he needed you. He needed you to fulfill something missing in himself. The fact you weren't his blood made him keep you at a distance."

"Did you have a relationship with him?"

"No, not like that. We were companions. We needed each other to make this work."

"I don't understand how Iron Crow could do it. I mean, it had to be incredibly difficult, and forgive me for being so blunt, Mom, but you were in bed with Foster."

"Of course, it was difficult for both of us, but Parker and I were in love. We did it for each other and we did it for you."

"Well, I'm glad things turned out the way they did. What happened to Foster? I mean, what caused his death?"

"Oh, I think in some ways he simply wore out. He had arthritis and it slowed him down. Then he started complaining of leg pain and back pain. In a way, I think his body gave up from all the years he pushed himself so hard. He ended up with heart problems. His age caught up with him. He passed peacefully in his sleep. He had asked to talk to Parker, and he told him he was grateful for all the years he had watched over the ranch and the things he loved. He shook Parker's hand and said, 'Keep taking care of her,' and that was it. He left us that night."

"I still can't forgive him for the way he treated us—especially the way he treated you."

"Maybe you don't have to forgive him, but rather appreciate the journey he gave us. Our lives would have been very different if it weren't for him and the ranch. He gave us an opportunity, Iron Crow and me. It happened at the right moment. And you, well, Zane, you were the gift." She reached over and patted his hand, and he took hers in his.

"Mom, it's so hard remembering all the things he did and wondering the whole time how a man could be like that. It never made sense." He took in a deep breath and let it out slowly.

"I don't know how we could have done it differently, Zane. Everything would have changed if you had known he wasn't really your father. You would have treated him differently and the entire dynamics of the ranch would have changed."

"I'm trying to take it all in, too, Mom. It's taking me a while to process it. I'm feeling like my whole life was a lie. On top of that, I've got this situation with Catherine and I'm torn. I want to be here, and I also want to know what's going on with her. It's tearing me up not knowing where she is and whether she's okay."

"I understand how that must feel. She obviously made the decision not to come here because she needed something else. What did she tell you?"

Zane picked up his coffee cup and finished off the last of it. "She said she needed some time to sort things out. I have a feeling I know where she is. She's gone down to where her family lives."

"Well, won't they take care of her and watch out for her?"

Zane knew his mother didn't want him to leave, and it was killing him being pulled in different directions by the two women he loved.

"It's the strangest thing. The whole time I was living with Catherine, she never got any calls or mail from her family. I know she has a mother and stepfather and she has a sister. None of them bothered with her. Oh, and she recently discovered she has a half-sister from her biological father. Her family doesn't keep in touch with her. That's why I'm so concerned. Still, I'm certain she's down there somewhere."

"Somewhere? Well, what do you think you should do?"

"I wish I knew. I don't know if she's at her uncle's house or where she is."

Maggie stood behind him, gently rubbing his shoulders.

"You have the weight of the world on these. Maybe you need to take a ride up to the mountains today to see what they tell you. It's going to be okay, Zane, no matter what you decide. You know I want you to stay here longer, but it's a decision only you can make."

~~~~~

Maggie knew everything was about to change. There had been a lone vulture circling overhead that morning while she was in the garden. She'd seen the shadow. It had glided effortlessly on the wind using the air currents against the pull of gravity. She could see the heaviness in Zane's shoulders as he carried the burdens of his current situation. She could only hope, as vulture used the earth's energy, that Zane would also find his valuable lesson through the energy of the Earth and the mountains.

Vultures purify the landscape, cleaning the environment and ensuring health and life for other things. They promise hardships will be temporary, so Maggie knew Zane would soon have all the answers he needed. Vultures don't even kill their own prey and are secretive. Iron Crow had told her it was rare for anyone to even see their young because they come from another world. He called them the Golden Purifiers. She hoped vulture energy would guide her son today. Whatever their true story, she was glad the lone bird had assured her all would be well with Zane and Catherine.

CHAPTER 5

The sea foam blew past Catherine as she stood at the shoreline's edge. Celia's visit had comforted her. It was nice to have a woman to talk to. She had slept soundly and awoke refreshed. The brisk breeze coming off the ocean was creating increasingly rough seas. She dug her heels in as the water swirled around her feet, sucking the sand from underneath them. It reminded her of days with her sister, Kiki, and cousins, Waylon and Justin. She looked down the beach searching for sand flea feelers sifting as the wave receded back into the ocean. The four of them had spent hours there playing in the water and searching for imagined treasures, sand fleas or crabs.

Her life had become like the ocean. One day it was crystal clear, turquoise, with the sun shining brightly overhead, creating sparkling diamonds on the waves. The next, it was churning, foaming, and pulling life right out from underneath you.

Catherine turned to walk up the beach as her hair swirled into her face, temporarily blinding her. She grabbed at it, pulling it out of her face, then looked up and down the deserted beach and screamed. It felt good to let it out after keeping it bottled up inside. It had been a hard decision to come here, but she needed time to sort things out. If the truth be told, she hadn't figured out a damn thing. She felt like she'd crawled into a fetal position and was going to stay there forever. Catherine knew it wasn't healthy, but it was easier than coping with indecision.

The only person she had reached out to was Celia, but why was she loading her up with all this nonsense?

Slowly making her way back to the beach house, Catherine knew what she needed to do. She couldn't put it off any longer.

Pulling the tattered small red address book from her purse, she dialed the cellphone. She was surprised when her mother answered on the third ring.

"Hi, Mom! I can't believe you answered the phone."

"Catherine, is this really you?"

She stifled a sigh. "Yes, Mom, it's your long-lost daughter."

"I doubt if you have ever been lost, dear."

"Well, I wanted to let you know I'm here in Jensen and wondered when we could get together?"

There was dead silence and then he said, "Where did you say you are? You mean you're here?"

"Yes, I'm in town, and I'd like to come see you."

Catherine wasn't going to throw Hamilton under the bus. Her mother wouldn't handle the fact she had been here for almost three weeks. It would be better if Hamilton told her. Or maybe he wouldn't spill that tidbit of news. She would leave it up to him. Her mother finally responded.

"I suppose you could come for dinner tonight. It's only going to be Ham and me, and I can have the girl fix a little more for you."

Catherine almost giggled. Her mother never addressed her housekeeper by name, but referred to her as "the girl."

"Well, I haven't been eating much, so don't knock yourself out for me."

"Oh, Cath, I don't have to do a thing. The girl will take care of dinner. What time do you want to come?"

Catherine glanced at the microwave clock. It was almost three o'clock and she wanted to shower and dress nice for her mother.

"How about five o'clock? Will that work?"

"Make it four-thirty. We can have a cocktail. I'll phone Ham."

Her mother and Hamilton liked their "toddies," as he liked to call them.

"Fine. I'll make it as close to four-thirty as I can."

"Now, you do remember where we live?"

"Yes, Mom. I know. See you soon."

~~~~~

Easing the Navigator onto A1A, Catherine headed south, passing the newly built museum and huge hotel, onto the bridge across the Indian River. When she turned left onto Sewall's Point, she was relieved part of the area hadn't changed as much. The well-landscaped sprawling lawns created a barrier between the road and the homes. Some had long driveways, some concrete walls and gates.

East High Ridge Lane made her sigh. Her mother had done well marrying Hamilton. He had made certain she and Kiki had everything they needed and enough stability to find their way in the world by providing their college educations.

She parked the car in the circular drive, walked to the large dark-blue double doors, and rang the bell. A short woman in a black dress with a white apron opened the door. With a Spanish accent, she said, "You must be Catherine. Your mother has been waiting for you. She's out on the lanai." The woman opened the door wide so Catherine could pass.

The house was spacious yet homey. Her mother loved old Florida cracker homes and had blended the hardwood floors and open country with an eclectic style of furniture. She had to hand it to Elizabeth. She was her own woman in many ways.

"I'm out here, Catherine. Please come join me. Hamilton's on his way," she called.

Catherine's mother stood as she walked out onto the lanai, and they embraced. She was taken aback by her mother's appearance. She seemed shorter than she remembered, and she was pale. Maybe it was her all-white hair. Catherine hadn't seen her without her hair dyed a rich brown. She was speechless for a few seconds.

"Mom, it's good to be here. I'm glad to see you."

Her mother pointed at a chair next to a small table. "Why don't you sit there; then when Ham gets here, we will all be close to the table, and I'll have the girl bring us our hors d'oeuvres."

There was a commotion in the front room and a beautiful black lab came bounding through the house followed by her stepfather. The dog put both of its front feet in Catherine's lap and licked her face before she could even put her hands up.

"Sorry, Catherine. It's not the way I wanted to greet you, but he got away from me. He's always so happy to be back at the house and away from my office. How are you, honey? Nice to see you."

Hamilton strolled over, grabbed the dog by its collar, pulling him off of her, and said, "Sit, Rufus." The dog immediately obeyed, panting with his tongue hanging out. Catherine laughed as she stood up to hug Hamilton.

"It's nice to see you, too. Lovely dog."

"Oh, he's a project for me. A gift from your mother. Her way of getting me to exercise, or so she says. You know."

"Well, he's lovely, and you are looking well."

"Yes, Rufus keeps me busy. He's still a pup; it will take some doing to get him settled. I'm still surprised your mother allows him in her house."

Catherine winked at her stepfather.

"Now then, Liz, how was your day?"

"The same, except for now. I'm beyond ecstatic to see my eldest daughter."

"I bet."

"So, Catherine, what are you up to?" he asked.

That was her clue not to reveal their secret.

"Well, I needed some time away from the farm to think. Too much going on there at the moment."

"I see. Always good to give yourself a change of scenery. Say, if you are going to be here a while, why don't you stay at our beach house? What do you think, Elizabeth?"

Her mother didn't show it, but Catherine knew she had never liked company in her house. Before they owned the beach house, they would put their guests up at the Coral Reef or one of the other local motels. Hamilton often picked up the tab.

"Excellent idea, Ham. Why don't you do that, Catherine? You could enjoy the ocean and still be close enough to visit. And what about Kiki? Does she know you are here? You two could spend some time together. Wouldn't that be grand? It will be like old times—you two little girls at the beach together again."

Trying not to reveal an ounce of emotion on her face or inhale too much, Catherine said, "I don't know about the little girl part, but it sounds splendid. That certainly solves it for me. Thank you both."

She and Hamilton had played it out perfectly.

"I'll get with you before you leave, Catherine, and give you the key and some info on the place." He winked at her.

It had been easier than she expected. Catherine let the tension go out of her shoulders as she sank back into her chair. The housekeeper appeared at the precise moment there was dead silence in the room, as if on cue. She placed coasters on the table in front of each of them, and then cocktails. A margarita for her and whiskey sours for Ham and her mother. The woman returned with two plates of hors d'oeuvres.

Hamilton said, "Thank you so much, Sadie."

"Yes, Sadie, this is wonderful. Thank you," Catherine said.

Hamilton proposed a short toast. "To family."

They stretched forward to clink their glasses, then sipped in silence until her mother finally spoke.

"I always thought of you as a margarita girl, what with you loving the beach and all. I hope it works for you."

"Yes, Mom, it's fine. Delicious, in fact. Thank you. How lucky you are to have Sadie."

"Yes, this girl has been wonderful, quite capable."

The rest of the evening involved relaxed chatter over dinner mostly about how much Catherine's life had changed, how long she might decide to stay, and what she would do with her farm. She tried to keep it as generic as possible. After a nice flaming dessert, she said her goodbyes to her mother, promised to return soon, and Hamilton walked her out to her car.

"Well, I guess we played that tune well," Hamilton said.

"Yes, I think we pulled it off. Thank you, Hamilton."

"Catherine, let me know if there's anything you need,"

"It's perfect at the beach house. All my needs are right there or somewhere on the island. I haven't even ventured out that much."

"Well, call me."

"I will. My next step is contacting Kiki. Tell Mom I'll call her, will you?"

"I'm certain your sister will be happy to see you."

"It will be nice to see her too. And again, thank you."

Hamilton kissed her cheek, then held her car door open for her as she got in. He waved as she drove away. Her mother had been smart to latch onto him.

CHAPTER 6

The sun began to filter over the mountain ridge as Zane Wheeler stepped off the worn wooden steps and strode toward the barn. He wanted to ride alone to think things through. He saddled up the same horse he'd ridden with Parker the other day, walked him out of the weathered barn and easily swung up into the saddle. A rooster crowed from the backyard as he trotted off.

~~~~

Maggie White Calf watched her son from her upstairs bedroom window. She braided her hair and tossed it over her shoulder. How many times had she stood at that window praying for him, and hoping someday to tell him the truth? That day had finally come, and with it, her son still in turmoil. She had hoped he would find peace at last, but now his mind was filled with his woman.

Parker came down the hall and slipped in behind her, wrapping his arms around her waist and snuggling into her.

"What are you looking at?" he asked.

"Not what, who. He rode out alone."

"He'll be fine. He's done this before," he chuckled, "and he's been fine."

"Yes, but you were always trailing him. Maybe you should go."

"He'll be okay."

"Maybe not."

"Let him be. He has some things he's trying to work out."

"Yes, and we are part of that journey." She sighed. "Did we do the right thing? I mean keeping it from him all these years?"

"I believe so. It didn't need to be told until now. I'm glad it worked out this way—that we were together and could tell him. He seems at peace with it now. I think he always knew something didn't quite fit, but I don't think he thought too much about it after he left. At the time, all he wanted was to get away from Foster. He buried it deep and threw everything into his work. It's coming out in layers."

"Go follow him. I want him safe."

"I know, my love. I'll go. I'll grab some things from the kitchen and trail him. No worries."

"I always worry."

He turned her around to face him and kissed her softly.

"Parker Iron Crow, you still make my heart skip."

"As do you."

"Now go before he's too far ahead." She pushed him away.

"Silly woman. I'm going."

He grabbed a red kerchief from a drawer and tied it around his neck.

"I think I know where's he's heading anyway. We'll see if I'm right."

He winked at her and closed the bedroom door behind him. She had been feeling under the weather and asked Maria Sanchez to cook for the men this morning. It had been the first time in forever she had slept until the sun came up. She turned and looked out the window as Parker headed across the yard toward the barn. It would be a good day for the two men in her life. It would be good her son and his father would have this time together.

~~~~~

Zane knew Iron Crow wouldn't like him going into the cave alone, but he allowed the gelding to make his way up the ridge. He liked the little horse his father had chosen for him.

Iron Crow had always picked his horses, even when he thought he was choosing them himself—like his first pony. The little horse had taught him so much.

His mind drifted back to the day Foster had sold his pony to the neighbor for his kids. He had been devastated. White Cloud meant the world to him. He had trained the pony himself and thought Foster had been watching him because he was proud of him. Instead, all Foster cared about was how much money he could make off the sale. That was a turning point for Zane. Something deep inside died when he discovered his pony was gone. His heart was broken, and there was nothing Foster could have done to repair the damage. That was the beginning of his desire to get far away from the man he had known as his father.

He reached a spot close to the cave where he knew it wouldn't be safe to push his horse farther up the loose shale and rock. He dismounted and pulled hobbles from his saddlebag, and bent down to buckle them onto the gelding's front legs. He remembered the first hobbles he had used made of deer skin and braided horse hair. Parker had made them and they had to be wrapped and tied back in those days.

Zane made his way up the trail, over the rocks past gnarled and bent trees attempting to grow on the rugged side of the mountain. He used a few of them to steady himself up the steep incline. He reached the mouth of the cave and checked for any tracks in case a cat, bear, or other animal was using it as their den. He saw a few small prints, but nothing to be alarmed about. Still, he wasn't sure he was ready to go in by himself.

Sitting in the shade, he leaned his back against a flat rock and stared out across the plains. It didn't matter how many times he experienced this view, it always amazed him. There was nothing but vast space and openness. An eagle soared high on the airwaves, silently keeping watch over its domain. Zane could hear his horse shuffling around down below, but couldn't see him. It was risky hobbling a horse in this environment, but he figured since it was the middle of the day, most predators were laying low.

Zane set his hat on his stomach. The wind was warm on his face as he crossed his ankles and folded his arms on his chest. It didn't take long before he nodded off. He stirred when he felt something tickling his arm. He rubbed it with the back of his hand and realized it was wet. It happened again with another drip of something, and then it began to trickle down. He opened his eyes and rubbed his face with both hands. That's when he saw the shadow of a man on the ground in front of him. It startled him, and he jumped up, turned around, and looked up above him to the ledge.

"You're too easy," Parker Iron Crow chided with a chuckle.

"What are you doing up here? You trailed me?" Zane asked.

"I kinda thought this was where you were heading. I'm surprised to find you outside."

"I wasn't sure what I would encounter in there."

"Animal or spiritual?"

"Either, I suppose."

"I see."

Parker slid down the large rock and landed next to Zane. He seemed as agile as he'd ever been, especially considering his age.

"You're silent like a cat," said Zane.

Parker smiled. "You should be glad I only have two legs instead of four. I could have had you for my dinner."

"I figured my horse would warn me."

"Sure, like he warned you we were here. You were so sound asleep you didn't even hear the horses greet each other."

Zane shrugged. "Lost my edge."

"Want to talk about it?"

"About what?"

Parker chuckled. "Never mind."

"Oh, you mean Catherine?"

"Sure, if that's what's bothering you." Parker was grinning.

"I've had a lot on my mind, but that's the biggest decision I'm trying to make. I don't know exactly where she is and I'm worried. I don't want to leave you or my mother, but I feel like I should try to find her."

"I understand your indecision. We waited a long time for you to come home."

"If things go well, I plan to bring Catherine here right away, especially with Buck's parents staying at her farm. That only gives me a small window of opportunity."

"I'm sure her place would be fine with the Matthews looking after it."

"I haven't talked to them lately, but her animals are pretty easy compared to their ranch."

"I'm sure Effie and Roan can handle anything."

"I think she's down south. South Florida. Where her family lives. It's the damnedest thing. They aren't even close. The whole time I was staying at her ranch, none of her family contacted her."

"So, do you think she would go there anyway?"

"I don't know where else she would go. If her uncle were still alive, I would think she was with him, but he's gone."

"So, when are you leaving?"

"I'm thinking very soon."

"Did you come up here to get an answer?"

"Maybe."

"Did you want to go in?"

Zane looked at the mouth of the cave and shrugged. "I'm not sure I want to risk it. What if I don't get any answers?"

"What if you do?"

~~~~~

Parker Iron Crow could see the hesitation on Zane's face. He knew it was time.

"Let's get some water from my saddlebag."

Parker unwrapped a piece of deerskin and handed a warm mason jar of water to Zane.

"Tepid water is better for you when you are exerting yourself. All these modern fandangle things. No wonder the kids are so puny. Put cold water in a warm organ and the thing doesn't know what to do. It shrivels up." Parker shook his head and chuckled.

Zane unscrewed the lid and took a sip of the warm water, letting it slide slowly down his throat. Parker took the jar from him, wrapped it back in the deerskin, and tucked it in his saddlebag.

"Follow me. It isn't far where we are going to the back side of the mountain."

Zane followed him around a small trail to the left of the cave's entrance. He hadn't remembered it until he turned the corner and stared off across the plains. The view took his breath away exactly like when he was a boy.

"It looks steeper than it is since the cut zigzags."

They made their way down the steep descent. Zane turned around and looked back up the mountain. From where he stood, you couldn't see the trail.

"It's over here." Parker pointed to the right.

A large pile of rocks, fairly wide in diameter, sat in a flat spot under an old black cottonwood tree. The tree was the only one in that area.

"I know one thing for certain," Parker said. "The day Foster sold your pony, everything changed for you. I could see it in your eyes."

Zane felt the too familiar lump rise in his throat. He tried to swallow. Pain slid into the middle of his chest.

Parker held up his hand. "Don't say anything until I'm done. One minute the tears were sitting on the edge of your eyelids welling up, but you fought them back, and then the next minute, your eyes were in a rage. I watched you in the night twist and turn in your bed, bearing the heartbreak of your loss. Believe me, I wanted to intervene, but my hands were tied."

Zane shuffled his feet in the dust, bent down, and picked up a small flat rock and started fumbling with it.

"It wasn't easy watching you change," Parker continued. "He had piled one thing after another on you, and that one hurt the most. Every time he hurt your mother, he hurt you worse. I wanted to tell you the truth, but she insisted. She insisted we leave things alone. I promise you it wasn't easy. Out of respect for her, I complied. There were a lot of things I wanted to explain to you."

Parker took a deep breath. "This may look like a pile of rocks, but it is a sacred tribute. I kept track of White Cloud. I knew it wouldn't take long before those kids had outgrown or become tired of him. As soon as I heard they had decided to give him up, I went and bought him. I went that same day."

Parker saw Zane's shoulders begin to relax, his body posture change.

"This pile of rocks hasn't been here all that long. Once I got him home, I turned your pony out with the herd he came from with some of his relations. What a time they had greeting him and him prancing and bucking. It was quite a sight. I came up here often to check on him. Watched over the years as things began to slow down. Then one day, he wasn't with them. I found him not too far from here. He was down. He didn't seem to be in any pain, didn't even look bad. I think it was merely his time. I thought about helping him take his journey, but I didn't have to. The old boy looked at me. I sat down with him, rested his head in my lap and told him all about you. All the things you had accomplished, how proud you were of what he had done for those other kids.

"I left him long enough to go to the ranch and get some things. When I got back, I lit some sage and we had ourselves a ceremony. I tied feathers in his mane and painted him up the way we once did many moons ago. The red was for his strength and power, black for his return to his home camp, blue for wisdom and confidence when he was sent away, yellow for his brave journey, green for his endurance and healing power, and purple for the mystery and magic the horse brought to our people in the beginning. I sat with him until the moon came up. A lone wolf called once and he was gone."

Zane didn't speak. He didn't move. He lowered his head and his shoulders began to vibrate. Iron Crow began to chant a song he had taught Zane as a boy. Zane suddenly was flying across the plains on White Cloud, the wind blowing in his long straight hair. Soon there were two voices rising from the back side of the mountain and two men joined together in their pain.

The sun was beginning to greet the horizon when they left White Cloud's grave and made their way to their horses. A small trickle of water was coming out of the mountainside; they found the two horses there, dozing together in the shade. They mounted up, heading back toward the ranch.

"How did you do it? Get him to the spot and put all those rocks on the grave?"

"I had to put a rope on him and drag him over there, you know. But I thought it was the right place for him. I worked the whole next day getting him covered enough so the varmints wouldn't get to him. Then, whenever I came up here to check the herd, I'd spend some time with him. It made me feel closer to you." Parker cleared his throat.

"I'm sorry," Zane practically whispered.

"Sorry for what?" Parker asked.

"For causing you and my mother that much pain. I should have stayed."

"You had to go."

"No, I didn't," Zane answered almost in a whisper.

"It was your destiny. He would have destroyed who you were. Now you are still that little boy flying across the plains on your pony. You are still who you were meant to be, and not only that, you took care of your people."

"I should have known. I should have taken care of my mother and you, Iron Crow. Those others weren't my people."

"We are all related, Zane. You know. You did what you had to do to protect what you believed in. All that matters is that you are still you."

"It doesn't feel so great right now."

"I know. We threw a lot at you when you came home. It's a process. Life is a process. You become a problem solver or you fold under the pressure. Your mother solved her situation the best she knew how. Sometimes I feel like I could have done more. One thing I know. We can't go back and change it, but we sure can do something about now."

They rode the rest of the way home in silence.

CHAPTER 7

The Grand Cayman rain forest was famous for its lush flora and fauna. James Delong couldn't care less. He wanted to be back in New York City, his beloved concrete jungle, not this sweltering nightmare. He had decided to run, fearing they would figure it out and find him—whoever the hell "they" were.

He was holed up in this sleazy so-called hotel on the edge of the nasty dripping vegetation. In spite of the heat, this was someone's idea of paradise. He didn't get it. Instead of street noise, he was listening to a flock of squawking parrots. Its only saving grace was the ocean. It brought him the slightest sense of peace to walk on the beach or sit under a palm tree sipping a margarita. That was pretty much his life now. There were people who would kill for this. Funny play on words when that was exactly what he had done. He had killed Roger and fled to the Caymans. It wasn't what he wanted. He wanted his life and his wife back, but reality had hit him hard. He slumped down in a lounge chair under the palm trees. A waiter appeared almost immediately, placing his drink on the small table next to him.

"Will there be anything else, Mr. James?"

Shaking his head negatively, James pulled a ten-dollar bill from his pocket and waved it in the air. The waiter took it and said, "Thank you, sir."

James had transferred money to a local bank the minute he'd arrived. The teller hadn't batted an eye when he asked her to set up the account using the name John James instead of what appeared on his driver's license. It was easy enough answering to Mr. James. He didn't give a crap what they called him. He didn't really give a crap about anything.

Who the hell would want to live in this miserable place? People checked in and checked out daily, and he watched and wondered. What the hell was the damn draw? You could go swimming in Florida for Christ's sake. Florida. Catherine's probably there. Down with her family—the family that didn't give a shit about her. Her family barely knew she existed. He had become her family. He was what she had cared about. He was who she loved. He emptied his glass.

The private chartered plane had been easy to procure. It had taken one phone call and cash. The pilot tried to interest him in several stops at surrounding islands, but James insisted on heading straight to Grand Cayman. He told him he wasn't interested in visiting tourist traps because he wanted to get to his destination as soon as possible. At times, the air turbulence tortured him, and he hurled out his guts into a bag.

Before the trip, he'd spent hours searching the internet to no avail. There was nothing about Roger Halvesord. Apparently, no one suspected he had anything to do with Roger's death. His little concoction had worked by making it seem as if Roger had a stroke. He couldn't even find an obituary. The frickin' nuisance was either six feet under or in a cardboard box. Either way, the son of a bitch wouldn't be bothering him or Catherine anymore. It wasn't much consolation for his current situation. Any way you looked at it, he was the one who had lost the most, not them.

The waiter appeared, interrupting his thoughts. "Another margarita, Mr. James?"

"No, no. Say, do you know where I can find a, well, how should I put this, a little entertainment—female, if you know what I mean?" He tried to smile.

The waiter stood there for a moment, then replied, "I'm not sure what you are needing Mr. James, but you can ask at the front desk. I'm sure they can assist you."

James waved him away. He'd take his chances at one of the bars tonight. What else did he have to do? Besides, the desk clerk was a little man with protruding teeth like a rodent, his glasses perched on the end of his long skinny nose. What the hell would he know about women?

~~~~~

The music at Tipsy's Bar was what James liked to call undulating. It was so loud it vibrated his insides. He'd never told anyone or asked if it happened to them, but he found it sensual in an odd way. It made him want to do things he would never otherwise imagine. It had started when he was in college, the first time he'd gone to a bar. He'd ended up with some innocent girl who found him attractive and had drunk too much. He convinced himself he hadn't really raped her since she had been willing to get in his car and make out with him. He hadn't stopped when she asked him to. It had been his nasty little secret. There had been too many others to count. He'd straightened up his act when he was ready to settle down, but now, well now, what was the point? The reason he had learned to behave himself—Catherine DeLong—was a lifetime away.

He spotted an attractive looking woman sitting at the bar and parked himself on the stool next to her. He ignored her. It worked every time. If you sat there long enough, they always struck up a conversation. He rubbed the moisture off his glass, swallowed the last of the Crown Royal, and pushed it toward the bartender.

"I'll have a refill when you get a minute," he said ever so politely.

She said, "Put it on my tab."

There was the lead in. It was so simple.

"Thank you very much. Are you vacationing here? Alone?" he asked.

"I'm meeting someone on business in a few days."

Fatal error, he thought. *What the hell is the matter with these women? Don't they understand?* It was as if she invited him in. He knew she would be easy.

"What kind of business?" He was thinking about the kind of business he wanted to do with her when she smiled. She had perfect white teeth and delicious-looking lips. She licked them and took a sip of her drink.

"Travel. I work for a cruise line, and they're thinking of coming into this port. Meeting one of the executives."

She wasn't dressed like a travel agent, and he told her so. "I wouldn't have guessed your career choice."

"Like I said, I'm scoping out the area. Checking out the type of clientele."

He attempted a fake smile as he stared at her cleavage.

She smiled back at him, picked up her bag, and when the bartender set down his drink, handed him some money and took a quick sip from her glass.

"Keep the change." She turned toward James. "It was nice chatting with you. Enjoy the rest of your evening." She sauntered away, disappearing in the sea of dancers.

If he had been younger, he might have tailed her, tried to persuade her to spend some time with him, but what the hell? He was nothing but a loser. He had lost Catherine, he had lost the most exciting job he'd ever had, and for God's sake, he'd even lost himself. Now, he couldn't even pick up some stupid bitch in a bar. He didn't bother to take a drink. He shoved the glass so hard it teetered at the edge where the bartender caught it and asked, "Bad night?"

"No, I've had enough."

James turned and walked through the gyrating bodies and the noise. He hated being alone. He hated the decisions he'd made, hated losing the love of his life, and worst of all, hated how he looked when he looked in the mirror. He'd done it to himself and he'd done it to her. There was no going back. Arianne wouldn't even allow him to crawl in bed with her. He had ruined that, too. She had been nothing but kind to him always. Hell, it was because of her he had met Catherine—the greatest damn thing that ever happened to him—and he had screwed that up. If only he hadn't listened to Roger. If only he had known, but how could he? The one thing he'd done right was finally to do in his friend, old buddy, old pal. Roger wasn't going to be bothering Catherine or anyone else for that matter. He had seen to it.

Blindly making his way through the mob of people on the street, James walked down the sidewalk. It hadn't dawned on him it was Saturday night and everyone would be in town. A bright yellow taxi was coming down the street in the opposite direction. He stepped out and hailed it.

"You sure you wanta go this way?" the man asked.

"Yes. Take me down to the beach, away from all these people."

"Yes, sir."

It didn't take long for them to weave through the mayhem and for the driver to deposit him at a pavilion near an old hotel.

"This look okay? It'll be a nice spot to look at the moon."

"This is fine."

James handed him some bills without even looking at them, briskly getting out of the car. He walked into the pavilion in the semi-darkness. Sitting on a picnic table with his feet on the bench, he listened to the sound of the waves crashing on the shore. The moonlight coming up at the horizon moved him in a strange hypnotic way.

He had dressed casually for the bar in typical tourist fashion—flowered shirt, shorts, and flip-flops, blending perfectly into a life he didn't want. He sat there for a long time and then he stood up, peeled off his shirt, belt, and shorts, until he was completely naked. He felt his body shudder, and then he walked straight down into the water, and when it was up to his neck, he started swimming out to sea.

CHAPTER 8

Celia was glad she didn't have anything pressing on her agenda. The drive to the beach was exactly what she needed. She pulled her car right up to the garage door, grabbed her purse, and followed the brick sidewalk around to the front door. She couldn't help but compare the differences in her life and Catherine's. The main thing they had in common was the same father—likely the best thing he could have done for them. She wasn't jealous. She felt a sense of wonder at how people's lives took the twists and turns they did. Catherine had simply made the decision to walk away from her life, and all she had to do was move into her family's house on Hutchinson Island. Celia stood there for a moment, then rang the doorbell. She and Catherine had both been blessed.

Catherine's dark brown hair was pulled over to one side, and she was wearing a bright turquoise shirt and jeans. She greeted her half-sister with a wide smile and a hug.

"Come in. Come; it's so good to see you again. Love your skirt."

Celia's flowered flowing skirt matched her rust-colored shirt and sandals.

"Oh, thank you. This old thing? Glad we could get together today."

"Would you like something to drink? Sit inside? Outside?"

"I'm fine for now. Inside is fine." They sat in the living room, facing the wide windows that revealed a rough but beautiful sea. "I heard the tides were higher than usual and it's rough out near the Gulf Stream."

"To tell you the truth, Celia, I haven't turned on the television or the radio. I've been kind of cocooning."

"I understand."

"How's your grandmother? How are you? How is Olivia?"

Celia kicked off her sandals, pulled her legs up onto the couch, and adjusted her skirt over them.

"Liv's wonderful. She's an amazing child. Stays busy. Me, I'm doing fine now."

"Now? Is it your grandmother?"

"Yes; Mimi really did give me a scare. I was worried sick she was in the early stages of Alzheimer's, but it turned out to be a metabolism thing. We thought she was on the verge of a stroke, but now she is almost back to normal."

They smiled at each other, and Catherine asked again, "Sure you don't want something to drink?"

"Would you happen to have a Coke?" It was comforting to be with her half-sister again and see how much alike they were. They used some of the same mannerisms. It was uncanny.

"Of course, I do. It's my favorite."

"Me, too. I've never figured out why it tastes so delicious and is so bad for you."

"I know. Say, want to take our drinks and go for a walk? The fresh air would do me good, how about you?"

"I was hoping we could."

Catherine handed her a Coke can and they walked out the front sliding glass door and onto the beach, staying above the wave line as they picked their way through the seaweed. A brisk breeze blew sea foam at them.

"There's been some tar, but I have lighter fluid back at the house, and some throw away rags."

"Guess you've been here, done that."

"Indeed. We spent a lot of time at the beach as children— my cousins, my sister, and me. We practically lived here. I loved eating food from the Sandpiper.

Catherine sighed.

"I sort of remember it, but we brought peanut butter and jelly sandwiches, so I don't think I ever went inside."

"It was one of my favorite places," Catherine said. "The wood was from the Martin Grade, and in the summer, it would get hot and I could smell the pine tar. It mixed with the salt, sand, and the fried onions. It was my heaven." Catherine started laughing. "It's funny what conjures up in my memories since I came back here."

Celia grabbed her hand as they walked along. "You can never go back and change anything."

"What about you? What was it like for you? Has this whole thing with finding out you have a half-sister sent you for a loop?" Catherine stopped, digging her heels into the sand, and looked out at the sea.

"I learned a long time ago not to be too surprised by what life dishes out. My mother taught me that. She was unpredictable; her life was unplanned most of the time. She lived spontaneously."

"I think I could be envious of that instead of my need to control everything."

"Well, there was a reason for it," Celia explained. "My mother was in a car accident on the curve by Mr. Wynn's vegetable stand. The car hit a puddle after a rainstorm and hydroplaned. Her friend was killed in the accident. Everyone thought she behaved the way she did due to the trauma of losing her friend, but years later, her new doctor discovered she had a brain injury—the part of her brain dealing with her decision making was affected."

"Wow. It had to be difficult."

"My grandmother must have known something wasn't right, but I think she was so relieved to still have her daughter alive she made excuses for her. Thank God I had Mimi to keep my life stable. My mother would disappear at times. She somehow connected with your father, resulting in me being born."

"Oh, I didn't know. I'm sorry."

"There isn't anything to be sorry about. Life deals you cards and you play them or you throw them back on the stack."

"You are such a strong person." Catherine reached out and touched Celia's arm.

Celia didn't answer. She pulled a small purple shell from a pile of seaweed. "These are my favorite. When I was little, I begged my mother to paint my room this color."

Catherine gasped. "So did I!" They giggled like two little girls. Suddenly, Celia started running down the beach.

"Bet you can't catch me."

They ran until they couldn't catch their breath and then collapsed beside each other in the sand.

"I think we needed that," Catherine said, breathing heavily. "*Being* truly is a blessing."

"I so get it." Celia slowly crushed the empty can she was holding and stuck it in her skirt pocket. They sat in the sand looking at the sea for quite a while.

"Well," Catherine said, "my life is quite askew right now. My husband turning out to be such a liar makes it feel convoluted and complex."

"I know it's tough."

"Did I tell you his mistress showed up?" Catherine continued. "I guess you could call her that, and she told me not to trust him—that he's not who I think he is. It frightened me. How did she find me? She drove right into my driveway at my farm."

"Seriously?"

"I know. Did she know he'd be there then? I threw them both out. I completely lost it and started screaming at them. I was horrified. Thank God my barn helper, Laura, was there. She came and stood with me. The plastic surgery he had to conceal his identity made him look like a stranger and shocked me. And then, as I starting putting the pieces together, I realized all the time Zane was living at my house and we were getting involved with each other, he knew. It hurt to find out they are both liars."

"Oh, my God. No wonder you came here."

"I hate it. I hated leaving my animals, but I was terrified. I didn't know who was watching me. Who could I believe? I didn't feel safe. And Zane. Well, Zane left for Montana right before James showed up. He went to make amends with his mother. He's there now. When he found out about James showing up, he wanted to come back to protect me, or come get me and take me to Montana. Instead, I fled. I was in my car at the gas station, bags packed to go to Zane, and I made a right-hand turn instead." She laughed nervously.

"I seriously don't know how I would have handled any of it either. It's a lot," Celia said, shaking her head in astonishment.

"Thank you for saying that. I'm not sure where I go from here."

"I understand about not wanting to leave your animals—your farm. It had to be difficult, but I also understand why you are here."

"I don't know how to feel. I'm numb. I keep waking up in the fetal position, curled up protecting myself."

"Armadillo," Celia said.

"What? Did you say Armadillo?"

"Yes."

"Oh, my gosh; we are more alike than you know. I bought animal medicine cards when I was here taking care of Uncle Walton, and the first time, I picked the armadillo card. Yes, I curl up like an armadillo and put up my armor."

"What else could you do when everything was coming at you? How else could you protect yourself?" asked Celia, shrugging her shoulders. "Who is staying? Taking care of everything?"

"Luckily, Buck's parents were visiting from their ranch in Montana. Buck and Zane have been friends since childhood. That's why Zane ended up in Highberry. He came to see Buck. Now Buck's parents are staying at my ranch, which is close to Buck's place. They came to visit their grandchildren. Twins: a boy and a girl. It's wonderful for them and it's worked out for me. But I miss my animals. I miss my dogs especially, but I had to save myself. I was heading into a big downslide."

"I get it," Celia said. "Here, let me give you a big hug."

They embraced, sitting there in the sand.

Celia released her and said, "Catherine, we have so much to talk about, and I hate to do this, but I have to head home. I can't begin to know what to tell you, but I am happy to be here for you as you are for me. Thank you."

"Why are you thanking me? I should be thanking you." Catherine stood up and reached out her hand to pull Celia to her feet. They both looked out at the ocean.

"Well, I think we have to be thankful we have each other."

"I agree. And in case you haven't noticed, we really do look a lot alike. I don't think there is much doubt about us being sisters."

"I know," said Celia, her eyes twinkling as they became misty, and she nodded.

They walked silently back to the house. Before Celia left, she handed Catherine the little purple shell.

"Keep this to remind you of today. Nothing is ever going to be the same again—you can count on that, but I'm confident you will make the right decisions. I'll be in touch, and we will do this again really soon."

They hugged and Celia kissed Catherine on her cheek.

"I love you, sister of mine."

CHAPTER 9

Zane called and asked the Park-It Storage attendant to charge the battery and have their mechanic do a quick once over on his truck. It would be shipped to Sanford, Florida, on the next scheduled Auto Train. As soon as Zane was certain the truck was in Florida, he would catch a plane, pick it up, and begin his search for Catherine. He didn't know how he was going to say goodbye to his mother. Yesterday, for the first time he or anyone else could remember, she hadn't prepared breakfast for the ranch hands. She hadn't even come down from her room until mid-morning. It wasn't like her and it concerned him. He had mentioned it to Iron Crow, who shrugged his shoulders and told him not to fret about it.

"One day, out of all these years, she feels a little under the weather and everyone is in an uproar. She's fine. She says she was tired."

He worried that all the years of his being away and her not knowing where he was or what was happening had taken their toll on her. Now, he had to break the news to her he was leaving to go find Catherine and bring her back to Montana before summer was over. He found his mother sitting in the sun on the back porch. She had a pot of green beans in her lap, preparing them for dinner.

"How are you feeling?" he asked as he sat down on the bench next to her.

"I'm fine. It was nothing."

"Nothing. I've never known you not to come downstairs first thing in the morning."

"I felt like staying in bed. I don't understand it myself. Old bones, I guess."

"Well, maybe it's time you allow someone to help you."

"I hate depending on people."

"You don't have to depend on them. You need to be kinder to yourself; that's all."

She set the bowl down on the bench and wiped her hands on a towel in her lap.

"It's annoying growing old. You look in the mirror and you don't recognize the person looking back at you."

"You look spectacular."

She laughed and took his hand.

"You always loved those big words. I'm so glad you came home to us. And before you say anything, I know what is on your heart. I can see it in your face and how you carry yourself. It's okay to care about someone that much. You deserve her."

"I want you to meet her, and I want her to meet you and see the ranch. I only hope I haven't messed it up."

"Then I suppose you will have to find out. When are you leaving?"

He sighed.

"Mom, you make it seem easy. I don't want to leave you, but soon. I'm having them ship the truck the guys gave me when I retired. It has a lot of equipment on it I probably won't need, but could come in handy. Plus, Catherine won't recognize it. I think I know the general area where I think she is in Jensen Beach, Florida. That's where her family lives. I plan to bring her back here, so I'll only be away temporarily."

"What about her place? I know the Matthews are there. Won't she want to go back there?"

"I'm not sure. I'm hoping, since they are okay with staying at her farm longer, she will come here with me first."

"You know I'm looking forward to meeting her."

"Only time will tell."

"I think you will be convincing."

"You have always had more confidence in me than I do."

Maggie White Calf laughed. "It's the easiest thing for a mother, believing in her children."

"I left you. I took off with Buck and I flat out left you. I should have stayed here and protected you from him."

"I was fine. I learned to live around him."

"You weren't fine."

"Zane, he changed after you left. He spent all his time with the cattle and the men. He distanced himself from me."

"He blamed you."

"No, he blamed himself. I don't think he wanted to admit he really had feelings for you. He walled himself off from it. He thought of you as his son, but he didn't have a clue how to be a father."

"How could you do it? Your whole life was a lie."

"We were young. We didn't intend to live a lie. We wanted a better life than living on the reservations. We wanted more for you. At the time, it seemed like the right answer. It worked out in the end. We are happy now."

"I see that, but it was all those years in between. It was the toll it took on you and the decisions it forced me to make. Now I'm worried about you."

"Zane, you can't go back and change it. You have to live in the present and be grateful for the journey that led you to today."

"I understand, and at the same time, I wish your life had been easier."

"It was easy enough, and now I am sitting here with my son. How could it be any better than this?"

He squeezed her hand. He would leave as soon as he received word the truck had arrived in Sanford.

~~~~~

Catherine looked at the clock. It was two in the afternoon and she had taken to her bed. How long was she going to do this to herself? All she had to do was make a decision, call the Matthews, and tell them she wanted to come home, but she didn't know if she was ready to go back to the farm. She missed her dogs, the horses, the smell of hay in the morning, but the tradeoff was being alone on the farm again. She hadn't called Zane, and he was obviously respecting her desire to be left alone. She hated to admit it, but she missed him the most. There were nights she reached across the bed for him, only to realize she was not at home and he was not there.

What was it going to take to bring her out of this conundrum? It truly was a bewilderment to her how she had let herself get into yet another so convoluted situation. She had trusted another man. What had she been thinking? He had made it easy to trust him. Was everything he said or did as calculated as what James had orchestrated? She had a hard time believing Zane was that deceitful. Yet both men had told her exactly the same thing—they had been trying to protect her. It felt like it was them she needed protection from.

The days spent alone on the farm before Zane had been distressful. She had tried to fill the void left by James' departure with the horses and the dogs. The busier she became, the less the painful memories knocked at her door. When she was bone tired, she would fall into bed and drift off. It kept the demons from haunting her. She had played scenes from the apartment in New York over and over in her mind. She pictured James' car careening down the ravine and bursting into flames. She recalled standing in front of the casket looking at something she wished she'd never seen. Now she felt even worse, knowing it wasn't even him. How could he have done that to her? How had he put her through the agony of losing him, allowing her to feel the grief to the depth of her soul, only to find out he was alive? Worse yet, he had been with Arianne.

None of it made the situation with Zane's deceit less painful. Weren't lies of omission still lies? He had told her he was waiting until she was strong enough to handle the truth. In a way, he was right. She had been left raw and vulnerable first by her husband's unexpected death and then by her Uncle Walton's battle with cancer. Both had certainly worn on her, even though she was grateful for every moment she and her uncle had spent together in the little house.

Even now, she barely remembered driving back to the farm after her uncle died. She recalled walking into her house and seeing Zane, but then there was nothing else in that part of her memory. Finding he had cared for her during her illness and recovery was shocking. She had barely known him, but he had come to know her intimately over those several weeks. It was appalling, and yet she had to admit she had grown attracted to him during the numerous phone calls they'd shared while she had been away.

Even so, it had surprised her how she had fallen so easily for him. Not that he wasn't ruggedly handsome, athletic, and intelligent, and beyond that, he was kind. What man would have stuck around caring for all those animals and her? She had to admit he had qualities she hadn't found in other men. Maybe in her stepfather, Hamilton, but certainly no one else.

She shoved the covers off and sat on the side of the bed. Yes, she did miss him, and there were certainly more things stacking up in his favor than not. Was it simply the shock of being deceived again that had sent her into such a tailspin? She had to decide what to do and soon.

CHAPTER 10

The searing pain began behind Roger's left eye. He felt as if his body were moving in slow motion and his brain was disconnecting. Nothing made any sense. He tried to open his eyes, but couldn't. He attempted to reach out, but his arm felt glued to the bed. His mouth wouldn't utter a single sound, and what he was hearing didn't make any sense either. It was as if his thoughts were pinging around inside his skull like a pinball game. He had no idea how long he had been like this, or even where he was. He didn't feel frightened. He felt like he was waking up from a dream, but he couldn't wake up. He was simply floating around in his own head.

~~~~~

When the ambulance delivered Roger Halvesord to NYC rehab, Dr. Finley had been cautiously optimistic, but by the third, and then fourth day, he wasn't looking forward to rounds. He knew the longer Roger Halvesord's coma lasted, the less likely the recovery. The fact the patient had suffered a stroke, rather than a traumatic brain injury, gave cause for some optimism. He was glad it was Saturday so he didn't have to drag a bunch of interns along and could get on with his day much quicker than usual. He almost bumped into a nurse coming out of the room.

"Morning, Dr. Finley."

"How's Mr. Halvesord today?"

"I don't know how it happens, but when I tell him he has to take a pill, he opens his mouth like a little bird and swallows it. Other than that, he seems the same." She shook her head and walked away.

Dr. Finley addressed his patient by his name and pulled his penlight out of his pocket to check Roger's visual acuity, refraction, and motility. The dilation and constricting function of the pupils surprised him. Next, he tested sensory function on the bottom of each foot, first with a cotton swab, and then with a tongue blade he broke in half. He used the sharpest edge. Again, he was pleased with Roger's response. He checked the bicep tendon using the reflex hammer. Again, there was an encouraging response. He patted Roger on his arm and said, "Well now, perhaps we are on to something. I'll be back tomorrow to check on your progress."

He paused at the nurse's station and told the nurse, "Don't put too much in your notes. I want to see if this drug will give him the jolt needed to stimulate those dormant pathways in his brain. I'd rather be guarded with what I'm seeing than give anyone false hope."

"The only ones getting their hopes up are the three of us, Dr. Finley—you, me and him. They haven't located any next of kin, and no one has called looking for him as far as I know."

Dr. Finley shook his head. "Kind of defines what's become of the human race these days."

~~~~

Roger was slowly becoming aware of his surroundings. He knew he was in some type of hospital. He was beginning to understand what people were saying. As soon as he was alone, he tried moving his arm. This time it didn't feel glued to the bed, but it did seem incredibly heavy. He tried again and was able to raise it off the mattress about three inches. It flopped back down when he lost control. Next, he tried moving his legs and managed to bend his knee enough to raise each leg up about the same three inches. He took a deep breath and slowly exhaled. He could hear people talking outside of his room, but he couldn't hear what they were saying as the door opened and a group of people entered.

"This patient has been here a while without any improvement, Dr. Finley. Do you think he'll ever come around?" one of the interns asked.

"The brain is a complicated organ. It is our connection to consciousness. We can't be sure about his state of awareness or perceptions. A new drug has brought a few people back to consciousness. I was working on getting approval to try it on him, but the quickest solution is to prescribe it as his sleeping pill. That's its true purpose anyway."

Another intern spoke up. "Dr. Finley, do you think he can hear us? Do you think he has that awareness?"

"It has been my experience that most patients can hear on some level. Some have reported hearing muffled sounds, but as they recover, so does their hearing and their process of language."

The student continued, "So he could be hearing every word we say, but he has no ability to respond at this time?"

"Great observation. Yes, he appears to be trapped by the brain damage that resulted from the bleed. The cells in the area have ceased to perform and possibly even exist as far as brain function. He's not in any real pain. Patients have told us while they were in that state, they were almost euphoric because they have nothing to do and no responsibilities, desires, or needs."

"Is this a persistent vegetative state, and do you feel he will come back?"

"Do your research. There have been cases where patients were trapped in their bodies for years in a vegetative state who later relate how they experienced their period of lack of consciousness, and then, at some point, began to wake up. Until then, they simply existed. One particular man talks about living in his imagination and having conversations with people inside his head. That's how he coped with his state."

A female student said, "It seems inhumane to keep him like this."

"Tell that to him. He would probably argue for life—that is, if he could talk."

"Didn't we, in fact, tell him, Dr. Finley? After all, like you said, he can probably hear us."

"Let's hope so, and let us also hope he decides to come back. The hemisphere that sustained the damage is the thinking side. He may come back to us as a different person in some ways. Or, he may have lucked out by having a left hemispheric stroke. He still has the right-side perspective of the brain, which is trainable and not all ego. He may relearn the things he has obviously lost. Plus, NY Med Rehab has the most qualified staff in the entire country."

"Good morning, Mr. Halvesord," Dr. Finley boomed, startling Roger, whose eyes snapped open as he turned his head to look at him.

"Well, look at you. Since a few days ago you were in a prone position with no responses whatsoever, this is encouraging. And, you have obviously gained some vision. This is all very encouraging. Nice to see you this morning. Let's see how things are improving."

Dr. Finley repeated the visual acuity and sensory function tests. Roger's reaction time had increased by about 50 percent. When he finished, Roger lifted his right hand off the bed and pointed at Dr. Finley, trying to mouth words, but nothing would come out.

"Roger, I know this is frustrating for you, but give it a little time. Your body is responding to a drug we started a few days ago. I'm encouraged to see things are starting to, let's say, wake up. You have lost all your muscle tone, and most of your bodily functions have been nearly dormant. We will slowly start you with some physical and occupational therapy and things should begin to happen more rapidly. We will also get you into speech therapy as that part of your brain awakens too. It's going to be a slow process, but we have an excellent facility, and we will do all we can to give you the maximum achievable recovery."

He patted Roger's arm and said, "We will start with some light work today. That should cheer you up."

CHAPTER 11

Catherine had chosen not to reveal her current situation to her family. So far, Hamilton and her mother were none the wiser. Neither of them had asked why she came home. She really didn't think it would be worth the interrogation to tell her mother. What good would it do for Elizabeth to know James was alive? Catherine didn't want to go through the story over and over. It was hard enough living it.

It made her sick, thinking she had spent so much time with James, believing he was her soul mate. They were alike and yet so different. He finished her sentences. He had been the best part of her—helping her see things in herself she had been afraid of. It was his urging and encouragement that had given her the courage to orchestrate The Missing Link Foundation. It had opened her heart. Those sweet little faces, the caring people she employed, the changed families—it had been fulfilling.

James always told her, "I'll give you everything you want and nothing more." She never said anything, but she didn't like it. She had always worked. He wasn't the only one contributing to their income. Now that they had been apart so long, she realized the relationship had been much harder than she wanted to admit. She had given up a lot to be his wife. He had lured a country girl to the hustle of New York City. It had frightened her in a way. It was too overcrowded with too many things to do. It had felt hectic. Maybe that was why moving to the farm had been so cathartic. It had brought her back to her old true self.

Picking up her cellphone, Catherine searched for her sister's number. She had no idea how long it had been since she'd seen or even talked to her on the phone. James had taken her away from Kiki, too. They'd been close as little girls, and being on the beach had reminded her of it.

"Hello. This is Kiki."

"Hey. It's Catherine."

"Catherine. Mom told me you were in town. It's about time you called me. I would have called you, but she said not to bother you."

"I'm fine. I wanted to find out when we can get together. I'm at the beach house you know, if you want to come here."

"I don't get over there much. I live in Palm City. Do you want to come here? I'll be around all afternoon. Why don't you come for lunch? You can pick up sandwiches on the way."

Catherine smiled. It was so like Kiki to organize her so efficiently.

"Yes, I can stop anywhere you like if you give me directions. I can't believe it. Nothing looks like I remember."

Kiki chuckled. "Yes, these snowbirds don't like where they live, so they move here, and then make here look exactly like what they ran away from. It doesn't make any sense, does it?"

"It's so different."

"I know. Okay, so did you come down the turnpike when you came?"

"Yes."

"Go back out like you are going to the turnpike. There are lots of places on the way to pick up sandwiches. I'm not picky. Anything except tuna."

"Okay, but then how do I get to you?"

"Call me after you pick up lunch and I'll talk you in. I'm off of Martin Highway; take the road we knew as Loop."

"I can leave in a few minutes, if that's okay?"

"No problem. We'll have lunch, and then you might have to follow me around while I do chores. We'll see."

"Be there in a bit. Love you."

"Love you too." Catherine was excited to see her little sister. Ever since their mom had married Hamilton, there had been unspoken competition between them as they each vied for their mother's time. Now that they were older, that wouldn't be a factor.

~~~~~

Making her way south on A1A to NE Causeway Boulevard, Catherine took 707 south past the Indian River Trailer Park. Lots of memories flooded her mind. There were times their mother had taken them to the Bait Box to buy bait, sinkers, and whatever fishing supplies they needed. Her father had worked at the trailer park as a ground's maintenance man. She drove past her old elementary school. She'd been glad when she discovered they had made it into an environmental studies center. It was where Celia volunteered and where they had met when Catherine was caring for her uncle.

Catherine stayed on Route 707 along the river until she passed the new park; then she turned up the too familiar hill. It pained her heart when she saw her Uncle Walton's street. She wouldn't allow herself to turn left. She kept driving. What if the house had changed? She wanted to remember it the way it had always been. She wanted it to remain in her mind the way it was.

Traffic is thicker than a school of mullet, she thought as she made her way toward Palm City. She pulled into a plaza and popped into a sandwich shop. Its outdoor placard had been sitting out by the road and said "Sub Shop." If she remembered correctly, Kiki loved turkey, lettuce, and mayo. She ordered an Italian Combo for herself and within minutes was back in her car. She turned on the ignition to get the air-conditioner pumping cool air while she called Kiki for directions.

Once Catherine turned south off of Martin Highway onto Loop Road, things began to look familiar. Besides riding in the savannahs in Jensen Beach, her mother had occasionally dropped her off at Pancho's Villa. It was a fairly large tract of land with an old farmhouse, horse barn, and cattle in the pastures. Miss Barbara, the owner, had a herd of well-mannered horses. She would take a bunch of kids on a leisurely trail ride and then, they would come back for lunch, which was usually Sloppy Joes. Catherine had loved every moment of it.

She turned right onto Hawk Lane and then right into the third driveway. The three-board fencing appeared fairly new, and the pastures were freshly mowed. There was a nice two-story yellow house with white trim at the end of the driveway. Catherine got out of the car, opened the gate, and drove through. It made her miss her own farm. She closed the gate behind the car and parked in front of the garage. She barely got out of the car before she was greeted by two large dogs, and saw Kiki coming toward her. The two sisters embraced while the dogs barked and jumped around them. Catherine held her sister at arm's length and they both started laughing.

"Oh, my God," Kiki said. "We sure have grown up."

"You're not kidding. Why don't you go ahead and say it? How did we get so old?"

"I have no idea. And why did we let so much time go by?"

"Here, I'll get the sandwiches," Catherine said as she opened the passenger door. One of the dogs tried to get in as Kiki called him back and Catherine grabbed the bag.

"I hope you have drinks. I honestly didn't think to get anything."

"I'm sure we have something."

They walked up the sidewalk and into the front door. The home was well cared for and decorated in a modern, yet cozy, style.

"This isn't all mine," Kiki said. "I'm a working partner of sorts. I'll explain over lunch. Want to sit out by the pool?"

It seemed as if the years had been good for Kiki. She'd had several careers, but mostly doing dispatch with trucking firms. She had also created an app the schools used to alert parents of emergencies and absentees. It had been her godsend. She was comfortable with her newfound financial security. It was a relief that both of them were enjoying themselves at this age.

"I'm managing the ranch. It's primarily a boarding facility, but we lease some of the stalls to a therapeutic riding program. It's our way of giving back to the community. We don't have to charge them as much as some other facilities would charge. It's a worthy cause."

"I think it's quite admirable. I'm surprised you're involved with horses. I didn't think you liked them that much when we used to ride with Tony over in the savannahs."

"I like the work. I like being outdoors, but I like the dogs the most. We are getting involved in rescues and rehabs of the larger breeds. It's fun."

"Well, I hate to tell you, but I've rescued several dogs myself. The farm was so lonely. After I lost James, I couldn't stay in New York. It made no sense. I made one trip to Northern Florida and bought the farm. I have about a hundred and fifty acres. It is really quite beautiful."

"It sounds wonderful. But then, Catherine, if you have all that, why are you here? I mean, what's up with the farm?"

"Oh, it's a long story. I got involved with someone, and I needed space and time to think it through." Catherine couldn't see any reason to explain the ridiculousness of her life. It was worse than reading fiction. Who could believe her life with and after James had taken such turns?

"I so get it. I'm not in a relationship right now myself. I'd much rather spend my time out here with the dogs and horses. Plus, I have Joy, my partner, if I need to drag someone along with me to an event. We are too busy on the ranch to be lonely."

They finished their lunch and walked out to the barn. It was shed row with two barns attached in an L shape. There were two arenas—a covered indoor and an outdoor dressage—but had fencing so it could be used for a variety of lessons.

"I've been messing around with some sorting. I enjoy it. We have a ranch nearby that has shows. My horse, Peyote, and I have won a little."

"I never pictured you riding. It's kind of interesting how we both ended up on ranches and with horses and dogs. And by the way, I love your horse's name."

"Thank you. For me it's about the caregiving. I enjoy taking care of them and seeing them bloom, especially the ones who are scared. It's rewarding to see them emerge from their fear. I didn't name him, my horse, but peyote is a spineless cactus. He was pretty wimpy when I got him."

"I understand what you mean about the caregiving. The busier I am, the less I have to face my problems. Speaking of that, I'm sorry but I couldn't handle anything else when I was here taking care of Uncle Walton. I wanted to see you, but he was a full-time job. As soon as I got home, I collapsed with a virus, and that's when Zane came into the picture. It's been chaotic since then."

"I know taking care of and then losing Uncle Walton took a lot out of you. You were closer with him. It made sense you would be the one they would call."

"Thank you for saying that, Kiki. I didn't want you to feel left out."

"I didn't want to handle any of it. You know I don't like to be around sick people."

"I kinda figured. And something else. I've been visiting with our half-sister, Celia, while I'm here. She's been a real comfort to me. Are you at all interested in meeting her?"

"Not really. I don't have much time, and it would add another dimension to my life."

"Her daughter, Olivia, looks exactly like us when we were her age. It's uncanny. She's tan and loves all the outdoor things we loved."

"Well, I'm glad it works for you, but I think I'll leave it alone for now."

"That's fine. It's up to you. I didn't want to burden any of you with my situation with James either. There's a lot to the story. You and I had completely different lives. We do what we have to do. I'm happy spending today with you. Honestly, my life is a mess. There's so much to tell, but I'm not sure it would be good for me to go back over it."

"I don't know if I should tell you."

"Tell me what?"

"Hamilton was worried. We hadn't heard from you. He was honestly looking out for you. He hired a private investigator to check on you. We know some of what you were going through. You could have called me. You could have talked to me."

"What did he tell you? I mean how much do you all know?"

"Well, we know James deceived you by being involved in some pharmaceutical mishap. We don't know all the details, but we know he's alive and right now no one knows exactly where he is."

"Hamilton never said a word."

"I don't think he told Mom. He briefly filled me in. He didn't want you to feel like he had betrayed you. He was relieved when you called and wanted to come here. He didn't tell Mom you were here, because he wanted to give you the time you had asked for. He had someone keeping an eye out for you, though, at the beach house."

"In one way, it makes me feel safer, but in another, it pisses me off. It's so like our family to do this behind my back. It's all quite distressing."

"It's not like that at all. Hamilton asked me not to contact you and to wait until you were ready. We are trying to respect how difficult this has been for you. Sometimes the way you want people to love you isn't the way they really do. Hamilton loves you and always has our interest at heart. You know that."

"Well, thank you for telling me. You weren't always my biggest cheerleaders."

"You don't understand. When you married James, I was devastated. You had always been there for me. I resented you because you left me. I acted out a lot without you, causing them a lot of craziness. You were so excited to be going to New York with him. You didn't know what I was going through."

"I never thought about it or you, honestly. James and I became totally wrapped up in our lives and were kept extremely busy. Then I started the foundation. I never . . . ."

"I know. I understand now. It's okay. I missed my big sister. We were always so close; then Mom married Hamilton, and suddenly, you were gone. It's what happens when we become grownups."

"I missed you, too, and it's been great seeing you, Kiki. Looking back, I realize how much James isolated me from everyone. I'm glad we can talk openly like this."

"Well, I'm here. You can come back or call me anytime."

"Thank you, Kiki. I appreciate that." Catherine glanced at her cellphone. "I hate to say it, but I better head back to the beach."

The truth was she was feeling drained. They hugged, and Kiki walked her to the car. As Catherine drove away, she watched Kiki waving in the rearview mirror until she turned out of the driveway.

CHAPTER 12

Zane knew he couldn't stay on the ranch day after day wondering about Catherine. Montana had been what he needed. He had made amends with his mother and Iron Crow and they had made amends with him. Now it was time for him to make things right with her.

It was a two-thousand-mile trip one way. He was relieved to discover he could fly into Orlando and catch a shuttle the thirty minutes to Sanford where he would pick up the truck. The flight would leave Great Falls; he would change planes in Salt Lake City, Utah; and arrive in Orlando, Florida, at about eleven-thirty that night. He would stay in a hotel and pick up the truck in the morning.

~~~~~

Buck was anxious to hear from Zane so he could tell him the news about James and Roger. What a strange turn of events. It seemed like ever since those two had decided to work with the government, their lives had taken a dump right into the shitter.

"Penny for your thoughts, hon."

"What are you talking about?" Buck sounded agitated.

"Oh, you seem distracted. You're usually making faces at the kids and playing with their food."

Buck smiled at Diddie, who was looking at him as he loaded up her spoon.

"Why don't you fess up and tell me what's going on in that head of yours?"

"It's nothing really. Not much at all."

"I don't know how you kept your job because you're a terrible liar."

"Oh, I need to talk to Zane about something."

"Buck, seriously. Pick up the phone. But before you do, you should tell me."

He didn't think it was important, but she wasn't going to leave him alone.

"Good thing you aren't working anymore, because they would think you were just plain nosey." He grinned at Deb.

"Stop teasing me and tell me."

"Damnedest thing. Catherine's husband, James DeLong—you know, the now James Campbell—has been shipped to a New York City hospital from Grand Cayman. Seems he took a late-night skinny dip and they found him nearly drowned on the beach. He's had some kind of brain trauma. Probably lack of oxygen, or some such, and they've sent him to a special rehab center."

Deb handed him two coloring books and a box of crayons.

"Here, you can entertain them and talk to me while I clean up the kitchen. That way we can all spend time together."

Buck opened the box and scattered the crayons within reach of the kids. He stacked up the plates and pushed them toward the center of the table.

"James nearly drowned?"

"I think he's pretty bad. And here's the kicker. The lawyer co-conspirator friend of his, Roger Halvesord, well, he suffered a stroke and is in the same damn rehab. How is that for coincidences? Karma? I'm not sure I'm buying it. A stroke. You know the story about how they were involved with the pharmaceutical company. I'm even wondering who arranged for those two to be in the same place. I'll call Zane after we get the kids settled. I can help with their baths, if you need me to."

"Perfect. I wonder what Catherine is going to think about all this?"

"Hard to say. She's pretty much detached herself from them. In fact, Zane doesn't even know where she is right now."

"What do you mean? I thought she was in Montana with him?"

"I guess I forgot to tell you. She never showed up. She called him and said she needed some time. He has a hunch where she is, but he's not sure."

"Doesn't that surprise you? I thought they had a great thing going."

"Yeah, I did too. Hopefully, she will figure it out. Meanwhile, my parents are stuck at her ranch."

"Well, I hope it works out for those two. You know I'm a big believer in love."

Buck grabbed her hand and pulled her down to kiss her before she reached across the table for the kids' plates.

~~~~~

Zane had everything packed in one bag except for a few toiletries he would round up in the morning. He would say his goodbyes at breakfast and head out toward Great Falls and the airport. It was going to be rough leaving his mother and Iron Crow, but, if things went as he hoped, he would soon return with Catherine.

He and Iron Crow had ridden to the back side of his favorite mountain that morning. It brought Zane peace to visit White Cloud's grave again. He had taken a bag of special stones he collected and began to place them in each of the four directions. Once Iron Crow realized what Zane was up to, he found a flat rock to sit on and began to chant one of his familiar honor songs.

Zane pulled a bundle of sage from his pocket, lit it, and began to smudge the area and then himself. The smoke blew over and around Iron Crow in a mysterious swirl.

First, he gave his gift of a white rock to the East—the direction of the sunrise and new beginnings. It had been White

Cloud who taught him the most about training horses and had given him new opportunities for growth and wisdom. East is the direction of the child from which he had grown and had become a good leader. He invited the Eastern spirits to carry his prayers to Creator and thanked Him for bringing him to this new day and his upcoming decisions.

He placed a rock to the South, the direction of summer warmth and abundance. It is the direction of the woman and he asked spirit to honor his mother—who had given him life. Then he asked for spirit's blessing on the woman he now loved. The rock he placed was a yellow sandstone. He invited the spirits of the South to bless his trip to find Catherine and to open her heart.

The third rock he placed to the West—the setting sun and the coming of autumn. It was with sadness he came to the grave of White Cloud and the end of his pony's life on this earth. West honors the Elders and he gave thanks for his mother and Iron Crow. He was grateful he could live his life in truth as they all could now, He asked spirit to help him with his journey to tell Catherine the sacred truth. The rock was a red piece of granite. It represented the fire in his heart for her.

The last rock was the North and the direction of winter, the sparkling crystals of tranquility and beauty. It was a message of strength to withstand the biting blizzards of life, and it is the men's direction. It honors the providers and protectors of the family and the nation. Zane asked for strength to face the upcoming trials of finding Catherine and convincing her to join his life for eternity. He placed a black onyx to the North. It was a symbol of release of the negative. He asked spirit to help him let go of the rage and anger he had felt for so long toward the man he had known as his father—Foster Thomas Wheeler. He asked to forgive him for selling White Cloud to the neighbors. He gave thanks for Iron Crow and that, in the end, he had been the one to rescue his beloved pony and give him this place of forever rest.

Zane's mother had taught him the meaning of the Circle of Life. He knew the ceremonies and the reasons she had clung to that part of her people. The hoop is never broken and always works in circles. The East gives us peace and light, the South warmth, the West rain, and the North the cold and mighty wind for strength and endurance. The sky and the earth are round; birds make their nests in circles. The sun rises and sets in a circle and so does the moon. The seasons circle around us, ever changing. Man's life is a circle.

Zane spun completely around in a clockwise direction, spreading his arms as if they were wings. Pulling a pouch of tobacco from his pocket, he sprinkled it in all the directions, inviting the energies of the universe and Creator to fill him with strength.

He and Iron Crow quietly joined their horses and rode back to the ranch in silence.

CHAPTER 13

A thunderhead lit up the horizon. It reminded Catherine of how small lives are in comparison to what was going on in the world. She remembered walking along the surf at night and watching the damp sand turn into a million sparkling diamonds. How was it possible to get so lost in your life that you missed the most simplistic, yet awesome, pieces of nature? How did you go so deep inside yourself you forgot how the waves sound slapping onto the shore, the sound of a seagull's cry, the smell of fresh seaweed, or the wonder of how a man o' war floats across the waves and blows up on the beach? She shook her head. She bent down and picked up a familiar olive shell. She loved them. They supposedly contained the alphabet. There was so much she had forgotten and yet remembered.

She wasn't sure about anything, except that she didn't have any answers. She didn't know what to do. She was lonely. She missed hearing Zane softly breathing in the night—the way he touched her, held her. He had been so tender with her. Not at all like James. Had she been so *naïve* to think they had made love? It had been all she knew, but Zane had taught her a different way of being together. She had never felt that before—feeling lost inside herself in those moments with him.

Catherine rubbed her neck and sighed. What had she been thinking? They had been so perfect. Nothing had really changed between them. It was all about James. He was the one who had set all of this in motion. His decisions. Had Zane really lied to her or had he honestly been trying to save her from the truth? Protecting her like he said? Wasn't that the same thing Buck Matthews had told her? Wasn't that part of their jobs—to protect society? That's what he and Zane had both done for all those years.

She took a deep breath. Maybe she needed to rethink what she was giving up by shutting Zane out of her life. Maybe she was beginning to come out of the shock of it all enough to think rationally. She still couldn't get over how different James had looked or how he had behaved. It was a glimmer back into the part of him she hadn't wanted to admit lay right beneath the surface all along.

And then what about Roger? Look at the so-called "best friend" James had chosen. A womanizer who had no loyalty. He was willing to sleep with her when he knew James was actually alive. What kind of a friend does that? Did she really want to revisit all of this?

She slowly walked up the dune to the house. She uncorked a bottle of Pinot Grigio, put some ice in a wineglass, and poured herself a drink. She stood at the front sliding glass doors watching the lightning play in the clouds until they rolled away and it was so dark, she couldn't see outside.

~~~~~

Catherine woke determined to change her mindset. She took a brisk walk down the shoreline. She didn't even allow herself the luxury of looking for shells or anything interesting that had washed up during the night. No, she was marching. Things were going to be different starting today. She would pick up shells on the way back.

Catherine walked all the way down to the bulkhead at Jensen Beach. A lifeguard sat in the stand looking through a pair of binoculars out to sea. It was early and only a few people were there. She sat down at the edge where the waves would splash on her legs and sifted her hands through the sand. She wanted a few moments in the familiar place of her childhood to let the ocean wash over her.

"Take it. Take it. Take it all away from me today," she said softly. "I don't want to carry any of this. I am not my past. I am not my past."

There, she had said it. She was not going to let her childhood or her marriage to James define her. She was staring into the middle of a large wave coming right at her when she thought, for a moment, she saw something. At first, she thought it was a fish, but then she swore she saw two arms. The person seemed to be struggling, trying to swim upward. She jumped up and looked and looked, waiting for the person to surface, but no one came up. She felt frantic. Should she run to the lifeguard? Had she really seen a person in the wave? No one reappeared.

Catherine waited for another wave to come in and then washed the sand from her hands and splashed her legs off. She slowly walked back up the beach, picking a few familiar shells to take home with her. She would keep them at the ranch as a reminder of this day, for she was determined to make it a turning point, but the image in the water bothered her. Had she imagined someone was there?

She took a quick shower, dressed, and hurried downstairs to call her attorney. She would have to wait for him to call back, but she had nothing better to do. An hour later, after a brief conversation, he told her he would do his research but felt certain she didn't have to worry about getting a formal divorce since she had a death certificate and documentation to prove the James she had been married to was dead. After all, he reminded her, the marriage certificate was "equally only a piece of paper." She still had a twinge of not feeling completely free of James, but she knew in her heart it was a matter of redirecting her thinking. At least now she could go forward without any doubts.

The next step would depend on what Effie and Roan Matthews' plans were as far as their going back to Montana or moving somewhere besides her farm. She was finally willing to start the ball rolling.

Zane said goodbye first to his mother. She took his face in her hands and looked deeply into his eyes.

"Come back to me soon."

"I promise it won't be long. I'll convince her to come."

Iron Crow said nothing. He merely hugged him and walked away. It was all either of them could do.

Zane's parents were growing old and he knew he had waited unreasonably long to come back to them. He knew the visit had been short, but he wasn't going to be gone forever. Not this time. He was going to find her. There was so much for Catherine to learn and understand, and he would convince her to come to the ranch with him.

The drive to the airport gave him time to think about what he would say to her—how he would approach her. He knew nothing about the place where she had grown up, but new situations never bothered him.

Changing planes was easy since the second departure gate was in the same terminal. It was a piece of cake, and his flight landed in Orlando only a few minutes later than the scheduled arrival time. He spent a restless night in a hotel near the airport and caught a shuttle to pick up his truck. Fortunately, his driver knew exactly where Park-It Storage was located. Maybe his luck was changing.

Zane thanked the clerk at the front desk as he retrieved his keys and headed out the door. He was pleasantly surprised when the truck started right up. There was even a half tank of gas in it. He hadn't driven far when he pulled into the parking lot of a convenience store. He needed a few things for the cooler and also to check out the GPS.

He hadn't expected the majority of his gear to be there, but it looked like everything was intact. Then he remembered the bag Buck had packed for him and the extra cash. He was again surprised to find all the money still in the bag. He would have to email the storage company to thank them once he got his life settled.

Zane grabbed a couple of bags of ice, some drinks, water, and a few snacks and threw them into the cooler. He found a thermal cup, filled it with ice, and grabbed one of the drinks. Might as well get on the road as soon as possible. He only had one more thing to do. He wanted to call Buck, who would probably be at the feed store by now.

Buck answered and they exchanged their brief hellos.

"I know, I know," said Zane. "I couldn't stand it any longer. I have to make amends with Catherine."

"What took you so long?"

Zane sighed. "It was my mother. She's slowed down a bit and I was worried. One morning she didn't even come down to fix breakfast. Said she was under the weather. Plus, I couldn't suddenly leave her when I was finally home."

"She must be okay now or you wouldn't have left. How far are you from me? Are you coming here?" Buck sounded hopeful.

"No, Buck. I really want to get to Catherine as soon as I can. Ideally, she'll forgive me and come back to Montana before it gets too late in the summer. I want her to see it now when it is at its best."

"I have some news for you and, of course, for Catherine."

"Well, what is it?"

"I had a call from Bill. The attorney friend of James' is in rehab in New York City—he suffered a stroke—a stroke of all things. And that's not all. James was living in Grand Cayman of all places. They found him nearly dead on a beach down there. He washed up on shore naked. The story is a cab driver dropped him off the night before at a pavilion. All of his clothes and belongings were found there. It looks like he took a late-night swim and was overcome by a riptide. The irony of it all is he's in the same rehab as Roger. They are both supposedly in bad shape. I guess your gal won't have to worry about them in the near future anyway. Should be good news for her, huh?"

Zane was trying to process what he had heard.

"You're telling me Roger's had a stroke and James nearly drowned and both of them are in rehab in New York City?"

"Yes, that's what Bill Brannan told me."

"Pretty damn interesting."

"Yeah, and aren't you at least suspect about Roger having a stroke? He's younger than us. Don't you think that's suspicious? Ironic?"

"I'm not sure I'm following this."

"Those two were the stroke executors for the United States government with their drug concoction. Now one of them has a stroke. Think about it. And, another thing—why was his dildo friend, who purportedly loved New York City, down in a jungle in the Caymans? I looked up the place on my computer. It's in the middle of nowhere."

"You go too deep into stuff, Buck. Give it a rest. You're not on duty anymore."

"Your gal is the one who's up against all this crap. I'm only looking out for you and Catherine. Are you sure there isn't something to all this? You know, because of their past? Maybe someone wanted to get rid of both of them."

"Well, I certainly wouldn't rule out any possibilities."

"I wonder who orchestrated putting them both in the same rehab. Doesn't it make you wonder? And getting back to you, why aren't you coming to see me?"

"It's not exactly on my way. I picked up the truck you guys gave me in Sanford. I had it shipped via railway, and I'm going to use it to find Catherine."

"Well, I'm bitterly disappointed I won't get to see you, but I'm certainly happy to hear you are going to use the so-called Buck-mobile. Please—and I mean it—please let me know where you are staying and keep me posted on your progress. By the way, my father is so impressed with your little black stallion. All he talks about is riding your damn horse."

"Well, good. Good for him and good for Trouble, too. Say, let me head south and I'll call you when I get a room tonight. How's that sound?"

"Safe trip, my friend."

A quick peek at the GPS and Zane headed toward what he hoped would be the beginning of the rest of his life with

Catherine. He was worried, though. He'd seen her in a terrible state after her uncle died. There was no telling what was going on with her, but he hoped to find out soon.

~~~~

Catherine called her ranch landline, hoping Effie Matthews would answer. She was surprised to hear a man's voice.

"Hello. Is this Mr. Matthews? This is Catherine."

"Oh, hello. Did you want to speak to my missus? She's out with the dogs at the moment."

"She can call me back or I can speak with you, Mr. Matthews."

"Call me Roan. You can call me by my first name."

"Well, Roan, I was curious as to what your plans are. I'm not trying to rush you or anything, but do you know how much longer you will be staying at the farm?"

Catherine heard a door shut and she could hear her dogs barking in the background. She was certain it was General's soft, deep bark.

"My missus is going to give these dogs a treat and then I'll put her right on the phone. Will take a minute. Okay?"

"Yes, of course; I'll hold."

She could hear Effie shuffling around, and she thought she heard Friskie jumping up on her kitchen cabinet. The familiar sound brought tears to her eyes.

"Hello, Catherine. How are you doing, my dear?"

"Hi, Mrs. Matthews. I'm doing okay. How about yourself?"

The exchange seemed so familiar it made Catherine feel comfortable about her decision to have them take care of her farm and animals.

"I called because I'm trying to make some decisions. I don't want to rush you in any way, but I was wondering what your plans are as far as staying in Highberry?"

Mrs. Matthews sighed. "This has been the nicest thing in the world for my husband. You have no idea. He worked himself to the bone night and day, and this has been such a blessing, but Catherine, you let us know what you need, honey. We can move right in with Buck and his family, if need be, or we can look around for something else. We certainly will miss your menagerie. They have been so much fun."

"I'm not exactly sure how much longer I will stay in Jensen Beach. I'm in my parents' beach house and it's quite comfortable, but I have to face the reality of getting back to my real life soon."

"I understand. We were hoping to spend the rest of the summer. When the aspen leaves turn is my favorite time of year, but like I said, we are grateful to have had this time at your place. We do need to get back and relieve our ranch manager. Roan's health is so much better, and riding Zane's horse has really brought him back around. And these dogs of yours. My goodness, they are something. I can't believe how well they all get along."

"I know. I swear they told each other they had to since they were all rescues. I do miss them."

"Well, honey, they are doing fine. Even Friskie. He follows Roan all over the house. The man has spoiled him."

"You have no idea what this means to me. Thank you, Mrs. Matthews."

"Oh, for Pete's sake, Catherine, call me Effie."

"Okay then, Effie; I'll keep you posted on my progress here and try to give you plenty of time. Thank you."

"Right back at you, my dear. Take care."

The conversation gave Catherine the peace she was looking for. She could take another breath and make plans for the next phase of her life. The biggest question in her mind right now was what to do about Zane. She picked up her cellphone and called Celia.

CHAPTER 14

Catherine poured herself a soda, hoping the caffeine would wake her from the brain fog she was in, and headed upstairs to dress. The sun was playing on the floor of the master bedroom as she peered into her suitcase. She really needed to go home or buy some new clothes.

She was soon driving south on A1A, hardly believing the summer traffic and the way the island had been completely developed. When she was a child, there were only three structures—the House of Refuge, the Sandpiper Restaurant, and the old hotel. The rest of the island was mostly uninhabited and a mosquito-infested swamp. Somewhere on the island, a guy her family had called "the dog man" had his camp, but no one had ever discovered where it was or knew how in the world he could live there. He drove a rusty, dilapidated truck and the bed was always full of barking dogs.

Old Captain Louis, who lived on his boat on the river side across from the House of Refuge and the couple who maintained the refuge, were the only humans at that end of the island. The remainder was left to the raccoons and an occasional bobcat. No one knew whether the cats swam across the river or used the wooden mile-long bridge in the middle of the night. It had also been rumored someone had seen a panther.

It was hard staying in the present. Catherine kept drifting back, getting lost in her memories. She had recently dreamt she was swimming in the shallows and found sea urchins and scallops. In another dream, she had been in the midst of some porpoise and they were pushing her toward the surface, but it didn't seem like it was really her. It seemed like they were pushing a man. They would break the water at the same time, take a breath, and then whoever it was would be floating down again. Some of the dreams made her feel weightless and wonderful, with turquoise colors swirling in the water, making her feel safe. When she awakened, she wanted to go back to sleep to avoid the world and her dilemma.

~~~~~

Making her way to Route 707, Catherine turned south, following Indian River Drive to Jensen Beach Boulevard. Even though she had shopped in the area when she was caring for Uncle Walton, nothing seemed familiar. She tried to watch the traffic and read the street signs, but suddenly, she realized she had passed her turn. She had to go to the next intersection and make a U-turn. It seemed like she always did that when she was upset about something. It bugged her.

As she made her way up Skyline Drive, memories flooded in. Catherine remembered when her family had taken that drive for fun with the car windows open and the summer breeze drifting over their sand-caked bodies on their way home from the beach. None of the cars had air conditioning back then. It had always been the four of them—Kiki, her two cousins, Waylon and Justin, and her. Somehow, they all got along in the backseat of the old tan car with her mother and Aunt Josie chatting away in the front. How she wished life was still that simple.

Catherine slowed as she approached the top of the highest point and gasped. It was a three-story Key West style house painted a beautiful pale yellow and nestled among native landscape. She pulled into the driveway and beeped the horn, grabbed her bag, and stepped out onto the tan pea gravel driveway. She wasn't surprised Celia had kept it natural. As she followed the path toward the front door, it suddenly opened and there was her half-sister standing in a flowing flowered skirt with a beautiful pink soft knit top, her rich brown hair pulled to one side. She had a hibiscus tucked behind her ear.

"Oh, my," Catherine said, as she approached her. "I can't tell you how happy I am I came over here. The view is magnificent."

Celia leaned in and gave Catherine a warm hug.

"Your house is gorgeous. I love it. It's perfect up here."

"You won't believe our good fortune on how we got it, but for now, let's put your bag up and go have our lunch by the pool and then I'll give you the grand tour."

Catherine followed her through the entrance into an open kitchen, living, and dining room area. It was decorated in cool turquoises and coral with beautiful artwork on the walls and lovely beach driftwood and shells sitting on the end tables. It seemed like she was in the Keys or visiting Ernest Hemingway. It startled her when, as if on cue, a large fluffy cat rubbed up against her bare leg. Catherine reached down to pet it.

"I hope you aren't allergic to cats," Celia said. "He's into entertaining guests."

"He looks like a male. Stocky. What's his name?"

"We call him Hemi after Ernest Hemingway. He's supposedly descended from one of them—you know, the six-toed cats he lived with—the one he named Snow White."

Catherine giggled. "I was thinking your house reminded me of Key West or Ernest, so it certainly fits."

"I try not to be too beachy, but it's so darn hard when you live up here and have this view."

Catherine stood peering out at a beautiful swimming pool with a low deck. She was pleasantly surprised to see there weren't any structures built in front of the house. It took her back to how she remembered Jensen with mostly tall palms and sandy patches of weeds and grass below.

"It looks so natural, like I remember."

"We own most of the land down there. It truly is a blessing. Makes me feel like it will be okay because we preserved our little piece of heaven."

Scared Truths

"I know what you mean. You must love it." She had always loved the wildness of their little town. The mix of palms, sand, and water.

"The only time I don't is when we have hurricanes, but thank God, my grandmother has a fortress, so we batten down and go there. She's not too far from us."

"How is she?"

"Mimi's doing remarkably well since she's come out of her medical scare."

"That's such awesome news."

"I know. We were so fortunate her doctor figured it out immediately."

Celia handed Catherine a plate and asked what she wanted to drink. After she poured their sodas, they made their way out to the patio. A warm, soft breeze swirled around them. The pool was impressive. It wasn't large but inviting, with several floating toys, and rafts. A nice built-in cooking area and a table with four chairs and an umbrella completed the patio.

"I always wanted a pool. This is really nice."

"Yes. Olivia and I certainly enjoy it."

"Sorry I was a little late. I didn't expect the west wind today, and the ocean was flat as a pancake. The fish were cutting through the bait and having a blast. I walked a while and watched a few sharks feeding close in. Loved it."

"Only you and I would get that."

It reminded Catherine how connected they were, even though, until recently, she hadn't even known her half-sister existed.

"The west wind does make the patio a little warmer than usual," said Celia.

"It's fine. I could use the time outside. I've been kind of hibernating all alone over there. I've chosen not to share what's happened with my mother or Hamilton. I'm kind of guarding what information I give them. I wasn't prepared to handle judgment from them right now, not even from my sister, Kiki."

"I understand, and I don't mind your sharing with me."

Catherine took a sip of Coke and a bite of sandwich.

"Sorry. I should have asked. You do like Italian subs? When you called, I ran right around the corner."

"Another thing we have in common." Catherine smiled. "It's giving me chest pain to go back over what happened, but I need to make a decision. I'm sorry if I'm redundant on some of this, but I'm really trying to process it all." She took another big bite and said, "I'm sorry, but this is delicious, and I honestly don't remember the last time I ate. I've been so distressed about my life. I want to do the right thing."

"I know it's been difficult for you. I honestly don't mind being the sounding board for you."

"Zane said he was protecting me, and he did," Catherine said, swallowing a mouthful. "Thinking James was dead was painful. Then that creep Roger was making advances on me. Zane helped me get rid of him. After I found out how much Zane knew about my situation and how much he had been hiding from me, I felt like I couldn't take any more lies and deceit."

Catherine took a deep breath, looking out at the beautiful river below, taking in the peaceful setting for a moment. You could see the Jensen causeway and all the way to the ocean. She let out a long sigh.

"It's okay, Catherine. You don't have to hurry," Celia said, sensing how difficult it was for Catherine to continue. "I don't have to pick up Olivia until three o'clock. She's with a friend, and her mother is good with them, so I don't have to worry."

"Zane and I were figuring each other out," Catherine said, turning to look at Celia. "We were working the horses pretty much every day. It felt fulfilling. I knew he wanted to go see his mother, and I didn't want to seem selfish, but I wanted him to stay with me. I understood he'd been away from them for many years and he really needed to go home."

"It's a hard place to be for both of you. I'm sure it wasn't easy for him to leave you either. Didn't he seem torn?"

"Yes, he told me he wouldn't go, even though I knew how important it was. His mother is aging. His father has already passed. Not that they had such a great relationship, but you know, he said he wanted to go talk to him at the grave. I understand. I really do."

Catherine pushed her hair behind both ears and continued.

"We interviewed and hired this lovely person, an experienced horsewoman, Lauren, who lives right down the street at my doctor's property and cares for her horses. She's perfect. She's knowledgeable, a huge help."

"Okay," said Celia. "Zane goes to Montana and you're on the farm alone, but with help?"

"Right, and Buck and Deb are nearby. Buck's parents were there from Montana to visit their new grandkids, so there were plenty of people to look out for me."

"I understand why you came here from our last conversation."

"Yes, it was awful. I still can't believe I fell for it. You recall I said James tricked me by saying he was from a local paper and he wanted to interview me. Some story about people changing their lives or careers. My gut was telling me not to do it, but he was persistent. I gave in, but the hair on the back of my neck was standing on edge while I was talking on the phone. I should have paid attention."

"I get it. Olivia has the same thing happen to her where she feels uncomfortable, and sometimes wants to get out of places or situations. She'll tell me we have to go. I've learned to listen to her."

"I should have known better. He comes to the farm, and immediately he seems oddly familiar; he even smelled familiar."

"That had to be weird. Then what did you do?"

Catherine had finished half of her sandwich. She rolled the other half in the paper and pushed her plate toward the center of the table.

"Well, I wasn't about to have him in my house, so I told him to come sit under the nice oak in the yard where I was sure Lauren could see us. We had barely sat down when he shocked me by revealing he was actually James—my supposed-to-be-deceased husband. It was gut-wrenching. It was like my brain came to a screeching halt and slammed into my forehead. I couldn't process it right away, and he kept on talking, explaining, begging me to forgive him. He tried to tell me the whole story."

"Oh! How awful."

"It was. Once I got a grip on it, I was furious. My God, I had stood at his casket looking at a—I'm sorry. I'll save you the details and forgive me, but the vehicle was completely burned, so what I saw was horrible. I had insisted on viewing him, and then it tore me apart. I spoke to him on the phone right before he crashed, or so I thought. I went through all of it—the funeral viewing, all the people, gave up my Foundation, moved to Highberry, and for what? So that he could suddenly appear and try to make it all go away? And he wanted to come back to me, back into my life?"

"It had to be such a shock," Celia said in a soft sympathetic voice.

"Then it was as if he accused me of doing something wrong by being with Zane. For God's sake, I had a death certificate. The government had paid me a lot of money in a settlement. I had his insurance payout. He was gone; I had grieved and then finally moved on."

"I don't know what I would have done."

"I was furious with him. I started screaming. All the pent-up feelings came flooding out, and that's when a strange car pulled up my driveway. It stopped and Arianne got out. I nearly died. There was his mistress at my house. I let them both have it. I don't even remember exactly what I said."

"I don't blame you. I don't know how you held yourself together all that time," said Celia, stacking Catherine's plate on her own empty one.

"Arianne was the one who introduced us, and I thought she was a friend. It was horrible, but Arianne said she hadn't come for him. She said she came for me. She knew he would try to contact me, and she wanted me to know he wasn't the person I thought he was, and not to get taken in by him again. I still don't even know how she found me, but it made me feel vulnerable that they could both show up at my house. And wasn't it strange they were there at the exact same time? Thank God, Lauren came from the barn when she heard the commotion and stood with me. I told them both to get the hell out of there and my life. I remember yelling at them to get out."

"What did they do?"

"Arianne never spoke to James, not a word. I don't think she even looked at him. She said she felt she had to let me know not to trust him, and she was worried about me, and she got in her car and slowly drove away. He stood there looking at me. It was him, but it wasn't him. He was never in that car wreck. He didn't die. And he looked awful and it scared me. I wanted him to go away."

"Then, he left, and you decided to come here, right?" asked Celia.

"Yes, because it was devastating to find out he was alive, had been shacked up with Arianne in Montana no less, and somehow expected me to forgive him for everything. I felt like such a fool," Catherine said, shaking her head at her own gullibility.

"I hope James understood how distraught you were with thinking he was dead. I don't know how he could have expected you to forgive him."

"I can't forgive him, ever. All he had to do was tell me the truth from the beginning. I would have tried to understand, or at least been able to discuss his decision making. He did all that on his own, and not only dragged me along with him, but Roger and Arianne too. He impacted a lot of lives with his choices. It even rippled into the lives of Buck and Zane, who both affected me as well. When I realized those two had known the whole story all along, it unnerved me. I was heartsick that Zane had known James was alive and kept it from me. When I called Zane, he wanted to come right back to me from Montana, but

I knew he needed to stay there with his mother. I thought I would be okay, but my house is big and, even with my dogs, I was afraid. I was afraid James would be lurking somewhere watching me. It was creepy even with Lauren there during the day."

"It would have been difficult to pull all that puzzle together. You couldn't have known."

"It was quite upsetting. Roger had sent me documentation when he was having his fit over me rejecting him. I read and believed it, but later, I realized he was only trying to put himself in a better position to move in on me. It was twisted."

"Zane wants to come back from Montana, you tell him not to, and then you decide to come here?" Celia moved her chair over out of the sun and into a shady spot.

"Oh, no. I packed my bags to go to Montana to Zane. Buck's parents agreed to take over my farm temporarily. They are quite capable, but it was extremely difficult to walk away from my dogs and horses. It felt ridiculous to be running away, but I was too scared to stay. I got in the car and stopped at the gas station by the interstate to get fuel. I sat there in the parking lot and called my stepfather here. He said the beach house was available, so I simply took a right-hand turn instead of going left to the airport."

"I'm sure it had to be a difficult decision."

"No, it felt like the right thing to do. It was similar to when I stood in the apartment in New York. It was only walls. It wasn't our apartment now that it was empty. Driving out of the driveway from the farm felt similar to that—void. I felt numb. Once I was on the interstate, I drove until I needed gas, and then I called Zane and told him I wasn't coming. He sounded stunned."

"I'm sure he was," said Celia. "Even if he hasn't been totally honest with you, it seems like he loves you."

"He says he does, but he kept so much from me which he said was to protect me."

"Catherine, I'm sure he meant it," Celia said, trying to soothe her. "He did the best he could. After all, you had been quite ill. I saw you right before you went back up there—you know, when you left your uncle's. You came to see me. I hugged you and you were skin over bones."

"I know you're right. I was so sick when I got home. Zane took excellent care of me, the farm, the animals. He helped me with Roger. He did so much for me."

"So, did you love him or what he did for you?" Celia asked as she stood up and took the plates to the kitchen sink. Catherine followed her into the house.

"Can I freshen up your drink? Would you like a little glass of wine?"

"Wine would be lovely, if you have a white wine, maybe over ice."

Celia filled their glasses halfway and walked back out to the patio, placing them on the table. As Catherine joined her, she sat down and pulled out her cellphone to check the time.

"Do you need me to go?" Catherine asked.

"No, no. Like I said, I have to pick up Olivia at three o'clock. We have lots of time."

"In answer to your question, Zane is a likeable person. I don't know what he was like when he was younger. He doesn't tell much. He never married. I know he's been with other women; he's too comfortable and smooth. Oh, and he's extremely handsome; takes care of himself. Helps with all the chores. He's smart and caring."

"You didn't answer the question."

"Are you're going to be tough on me?"

"Not tough. Trying to get you to say it."

Celia leaned forward and picked up a seashell from a bowl on the table. She gently rubbed it between her fingers.

"Okay, I'll say it. I truly had feelings for him."

"Had? Is that past tense?" asked Celia.

"I don't know how I feel right now. I'm conflicted."

"So, tell me what made you have feelings for him, besides what you told me a minute ago. Was there an attraction? Chemistry?"

"It's kind of embarrassing to admit it. James was my only experience until this happened. I was so committed to my education, my friends. I mean I dated, but I was one of those girls who had my priorities in order. I was waiting for the man I would marry."

"Exactly what are you saying, Catherine? Zane made you feel things you had never felt with James?"

"Damn, you're good at this. You're going to get me to admit I love him. Is that it?"

"Well, do you?"

Catherine's face became flushed, and she could feel heat in her cheeks moving all the way down her neck. Celia giggled at Catherine's reaction.

"Okay, then. It's obvious the effect this guy has on you. Emotions. We're finally getting somewhere."

Catherine couldn't hold them back. Tears started pouring out as she held her face in her hands.

"I'm sorry. I'm so sorry. I didn't want to do this."

"Are you kidding?" Celia asked, her eyes growing wide. "Catherine, look at what you've been through. Did you ever really let yourself cry? I doubt it."

Catherine sobbed and tried to catch her breath. Celia stood and pulled her up out of her chair and wrapped her arms around her.

"Catherine, it's okay to let it out. You are safe here. Let it all go."

Catherine cried and cried while Celia held her and then handed her a box of tissues. She blew her nose and dabbed her blood-red eyes as she blinked and blinked, trying to get her contact back where it belonged.

"It's wrong to dump all this on you. This was supposed to be a nice afternoon of getting to know each other." She blew her nose really hard.

"Who made those rules? Certainly not me."

"I feel so needy."

"Needy? No, you should feel so human. Life happens. I've had enough experience with friends and counseling to know that even though you don't want to admit it, this Zane guy really has a hold on your heart."

"I don't want to say it."

"Then don't, but it's pretty clear you have deep feelings for him."

"He made me feel like no one else can, and he gets me. And not only that—he's kind and smart and my animals love him, but there is still my underlying doubt."

"Are you finally getting closer to answering your own questions?"

"Yes, I guess I am. I do want to go to Montana and see what happens, but I don't know when to go, and I haven't even spoken to him for a while."

"What are you going to do?" Celia asked as she sat down.

"I want to wait a few more days, but I don't know why. I think I need to wait."

Catherine pulled the chair out further from the table and sat down.

"Then wait, but not too much longer."

"I don't think he's going anywhere. He can't go to my house in Highberry until the Matthews are ready to leave, and he doesn't know where I am."

"I bet he has a pretty good idea; don't you?"

"Maybe. I don't know. I doubt it."

"So do you feel safe at the beach?"

"Yes, I do. I don't think James is clever enough to find me here. He doesn't have the connections like he used to."

"Well, then you should relax and enjoy yourself. Catch your breath."

"I try, but I keep rethinking everything."

"I hate when I do that. It accomplishes nothing."

"Can you say it fourteen times?"

"What?"

"You know—the part about rethinking everything accomplishes nothing."

"You're too funny. You've already crossed so many bridges. This should be much easier for you. You are going to someone who loves you, and it sounds like you love him. Love should be easy, don't you think?"

"I always had to work hard at it with James. I didn't realize it until now. I really need to go." Catherine stood, walked into the kitchen, and put the remaining half of her sandwich back in the bag.

"I'll eat the rest of this for dinner."

"Yes, you should. I'll walk you out."

They embraced. Celia hugged her softly, yet reassuringly.

"You are a special person, Catherine. Don't let anyone change who you are," Celia said, looking her in the eye as she let go of her.

"Thank you, Celia. You have given me clarity."

"My pleasure, but I assure you, it was all you."

CHAPTER 15

Zane shouldn't have worried about what shape the truck would be in when he picked it up, even though it had seemed like a thorn in his side. He knew Buck had been the mastermind behind his cohorts giving it to him as his retirement gift. Ever since he had saved his best friend's life, Buck had felt like he owed him something. The truck looked like any common full-size truck, but it would give him visibility and at the same time blend in. It had a V8 engine, so he had plenty of power. The seats were fairly comfortable for the haul or sitting for long periods on surveillance through the darkly tinted windows.

He was feeling anxious about exactly what he would find when he arrived in Jensen Beach, but right now it would be his best bet for locating Catherine without her knowing he was stalking her.

The drive reminded Zane of how much he disliked south Florida. The truck handled well enough, but he missed the steady purr of his diesel. He would arrive in plenty of daylight to locate a room and scope out some of the area. Then he'd get to work. It would be easy with his connections to locate her family and all their information. The USB port in the truck dash enabled him to charge the laptop while he drove. Things seemed to be falling into place. Now all he had to do was find Catherine.

He couldn't comprehend why people wanted to live in a concrete jungle. From the looks of it, they wouldn't be happy until every inch of the state was covered in buildings and parking lots. The GPS was mounted in the center console. He had turned the volume down because he couldn't stand the screechy female voice they used.

"Exit right number 133 off of Florida turnpike," she chirped. Any other time, he wouldn't have even been on a major highway, but today, he was hell-bent on making time. The sooner he got there, the quicker he could find her and try to explain it all away. Most of all, he wanted to hold her in his arms, smell the sweetness of her hair, and feel her close to him again.

It had been gut-wrenching to say goodbye to his mother and Iron Crow. His mother was moving much slower than he remembered. Her allowing Maria to help her in the kitchen was something he thought she would never do, but she said her legs ached when she stood for long periods of time. He hoped he wouldn't be gone long before Catherine would agree to make the trip back to Montana with him.

Veering right off the turnpike, Zane paid his toll and glanced at the GPS. He was to continue straight through Palm City. It was a four-lane road bordered by housing developments, shopping centers, and gas stations. He slowly made his way toward Stuart and over what appeared to be a fairly new bridge headed toward Jensen Beach. Once he'd bedded down for the night, he would spend some time researching and mapping out his strategy for boxing her in.

He pulled off the road into a gas station and turned on the laptop. One reason he had been relieved to bail from service was because the world had become so techno. Now, here he was once again using a damn computer. He searched for old motels in Jensen Beach hoping to find someplace small and secluded away from the big hotel chains.

Heading north on Indian River Drive, Zane pulled into the Seaglass Motel's parking lot. It overlooked a fairly wide section of the river and was north of the Jensen Beach causeway. It didn't take long to secure a room, since it was the dead of summer and their off-season. The clerk told him he had picked the perfect time if he wanted some peace and quiet.

The room was clean and efficient, including a small refrigerator. He didn't unpack a thing, but instead headed right back out to find a place to eat. He didn't really plan on staying all that long.

~~~~

It was the first time Catherine had considered calling Zane. She had her cellphone in her pocket and was sitting in front of the beach house under an umbrella. It was simple—dial the phone. She had a knot in her stomach, and she wasn't sure she would find her voice. She pulled the phone from her back jeans pocket and sat holding it in her hand. It wasn't even turned on. The last time she'd used it was to call Celia.

Catherine didn't know how he would react after not hearing from her for such a long time. She knew summer was quickly passing and her opportunity to go to him in Montana was fleeting as well. It was now or never. Do or die. Oh, how she had learned to hate that phrase. Look at what James had done. He had basically killed both of their lives. She let out a long sigh through her nose. She had her jaw clenched so tightly it was hurting her teeth.

"Just do it. Do it right now," she whispered to herself. She slowly turned on her cellphone and found Zane's number. She didn't even recall the last time she had spoken with him. She was about to end the call when he answered. She couldn't get her mouth to move or words to come out.

"Hello. Catherine, are you there? Catherine, say something. I know it's you. Talk to me."

She finally found the strength to say "Hello, Zane. How are you?"

"Oh, Catherine, I'm so glad it's really you. I have been worried sick."

"It's me all right. So, how are you?" She asked again nervously.

"Well, it's not so important how I am. How are you? Where are you? I've been scared for you."

"I'm in a safe place. You shouldn't worry. I'm quite okay. Resting. Trying to get my bearings. You know."

"No, I can't pretend to know how you feel. I've been trying to understand what you must be going through. Honestly, I want to see you, talk to you, explain to you what——"

"Explain?" said Catherine curtly. "That's exactly what James tried to do. It must be a male trait. You guys say you don't talk much, but it seems to me that's all any of you want to do. Maybe for once you should listen. Maybe you should have heard what I was trying to say."

She hadn't meant to sound so angry.

~~~~

Zane wasn't surprised Catherine was so reactionary. He had expected it. That's why he wanted to see her in person. If he could see her, address her with his body posture, instead of discussing this over the phone, maybe he would have a better chance.

"I can't blame you at all for feeling the way you do. You have the right to be angry. I understand. Truly, I do."

He heard her sigh, the sigh he had heard while she was healing. He was worried she might be back in that state of mind again.

"I'm not trying to push you. Can I come to you? Be there for you? I will do it. I will come right away."

"I don't know if I'm ready, Zane. I don't know what I want."

Every ounce of him wanted to blurt out he was right there—a lot nearer than she could imagine—and he was ready to meet her anywhere she chose in Jensen Beach. He was right there, but he couldn't predict her reaction to that either. He'd have to bide his time patiently, something he'd had to learn in his profession.

"I'll wait. I can be as patient as you need me to be," he said, trying to reassure her.

"How is Montana? Your mother? Is everything okay there?"

"Montana is fine. My mother was a little under the weather, feeling her age, I guess. I don't know for sure, but overall, it's all good."

As soon as he said the word "was," he wished he hadn't, but she didn't seem to notice—hadn't suspected he wasn't in Montana.

"Zane, you know things moved fairly fast for us. Maybe it was too fast. You have to know I have feelings for you."

"Yes, as do I for you."

"Well, I need some time to sort this out, even though I'm really missing my dogs and horses. In a lot of ways, I wish I could be home."

"I understand. I'd like to be back there, too."

"Well, besides the issue with James, I have the matter of the Matthews. I don't want to kick them out. Effie said they'd like to be back at their ranch before the snow starts, so I only have a little time."

"Yes, so what are you telling me?"

"I'll let you know something soon. I promise."

"Okay," said Zane, though he didn't like to wait. "Will you call me then? Soon?"

"Yes, of course I will. I'll call you soon."

He was fighting the impulse to tell her he wanted to meet her right then, to know where she was, to find her and make it okay between them.

"Are you going to tell me where you are so I can at least not worry about you?"

"You don't have to worry, Zane. I'm in a safe place. I don't think James will find me here."

He didn't want to push too hard, but it was killing him. He also didn't want to tell her about James and Roger over the phone, because he didn't know how she would react. He was so close, but he knew her well enough to back off. She was damn independent and could be headstrong.

"Catherine, you do know I love you, don't you?"

"Zane, I do believe you, but I don't know if that's what I want to hear right now. I have to go."

~~~~~

Catherine suddenly felt drained. It had taken all the willpower she could muster not to cave. Part of her wanted to tell Zane to come and get her—to tell him how she had been so afraid the first few nights alone at the beach. She had slept in a fetal position all curled up like an armadillo, protecting herself from what she feared would come. She wanted to share the dreams she had of swimming and swimming and swimming—how she felt like she had been swept out to sea and was drowning, drowning, drowning. But she didn't. She kept it all locked up tight inside, not wanting him to think she was weak.

She didn't expect Zane to be her knight in shining armor who rescued the damsel in distress. She wanted to be strong and brave again. She longed to feel safe and secure and like no one and nothing could come and hurt her, but she still felt vulnerable. Men had betrayed her—lied to her. He had come and rescued her from Roger, from the pain of losing James, from the fear of being unattractive and unloved again. He had been slow and steady; quietly swept her off her feet, but she needed to find herself again.

Their romance had been the kind she had read about or watched on the big screen. The first time he made love to her, she had held back, but honestly, if she had let herself feel what she was really feeling, she would have nearly turned inside out. He had been so careful and slow and easy. It had been a dream walk into a place she had never been before—all mist and fog swirling around and hot and steamy at the same time. In fact, she had been so hot she thought she was going to pass out, but then had reached a place she'd never felt before. She screamed out loud and his mouth had found hers and quieted her. She'd felt what she thought were tears falling on her cheek from him as he kissed her. At first, his lips were soft and tender, and then his tongue had found hers. She felt her own tears begin to slide helplessly down her cheeks. Could it have been the moment she had fallen so much in love with him?

Catherine didn't want to feel what she was feeling deep inside. She had been holding herself so tightly her arms began to ache. She was shaking. She had to make a decision and soon—couldn't keep on living in this limbo.

"I have to get out of here," she told herself.

Catherine dressed in her favorite purple shirt and pulled on a nice pair of jeans. She wished she'd brought some jewelry, but she hadn't even thought of it when she had hurriedly packed after the horrible encounter with James and Arianne. There was one place that always made her feel better. She backed the car out of the garage, used the remote to close the door, and headed toward the bookstore.

The beach house was close to the causeway on the island. She made her way east across it, and then south to Jensen Beach Boulevard. She would head west to the highway and, if she remembered correctly, the bookstore should be on the right. She glanced in her mirrors periodically, keeping track of the vehicles around her. If Zane had taught her anything, it was to be aware of her surroundings. After what James had been involved in, and what Zane had done for a living, she had become almost too aware her life held much more danger than she had ever imagined.

It didn't take long for her to realize a white pickup truck seemed to be mimicking her every move. She erratically pulled into a gas station and when the truck passed on by, she pulled back out into traffic, keeping an eye out for the truck. As she parked at the bookstore, she didn't notice anything unusual.

Grabbing her purse, Catherine dashed toward the store, following a family inside, something Zane had also taught her. He had told her if she was going to exit her car and go into a store, to be sure someone else was also in the parking lot, and it would be a lot safer if she followed a family. That way, no one would be as apt to try to grab her or do anything. It had felt unnecessary at the time, but now she was finding his information quite useful.

Catherine headed straight for the magazine rack, looking for a particular publication she had enjoyed in the past. It was about cowboys and Indians with beautiful advertisements, and excellent articles about Native Americans. She had missed having the monthly issues. She also picked up a magazine on writing. It certainly wouldn't hurt to hone in on her skills while she had a little time on her hands. She made her way to the checkout counter, paid for her purchase, and headed to the parking lot behind an elderly couple. They were walking arm in arm slowly in front of her.

Glancing around, Catherine was startled when she saw a white pickup truck parked not three spaces from her Lincoln. She couldn't believe it. It looked like the same truck, with the windows darkened. She hurried across the parking lot, entered her vehicle locking the doors before she even got the driver's door completely closed. She shoved the key in the ignition. She almost gave it too much gas and the engine kind of roared as she looked behind her and backed out of the parking space.

She was sitting at the traffic light, waiting to make a left-hand turn, when the truck came up alongside her, also in a left-hand turn lane. They would be making the turn together. She didn't want to be obvious, so she tried to look out of the corner of her eye like she had seen Zane do many times.

The damn truck windows were so dark she couldn't tell who was driving. It made her feel nervous, but the light changed and she was the lead car, so she sped away. When she looked in her rearview mirror, the truck was making a slower exit from the light. She turned, heading east, and tried to hide herself by changing lanes several times. She glanced behind her, using all three mirrors, and couldn't find the truck. Back at the beach house, she wasted no time getting the car into the garage, shutting the door, and entering the house through the inside door. She checked all the interior doors to be sure they were locked, then ran upstairs, and looked out the back window to see if she could see anything suspicious. The driveway was clear, and the view she had of the street didn't reveal anything. She exhaled. Maybe she was trying to make this into something it wasn't. All she wanted to do was relax and get her mind off things for a little while.

Fixing herself a glass of soda, Catherine decided to stay inside the locked house for her peace of mind. It was late afternoon anyway, and she really didn't care to be outside if the no-see-ums decided they needed a feeding frenzy. *"It's all going to be okay. You'll see,"* she told herself. She immersed her mind into looking at beautiful Western dresses, cowboy boots, and an article about Native American artists. Before long, the magazine fell out of her hands when she drifted off to sleep.

~~~~

Zane hadn't wanted to spook Catherine, and he was pissed he'd lost her in the damn traffic. It wasn't his style. Martin County tax records revealed one property owned by Hamilton Wesley and Elizabeth Howell. It wasn't likely she'd be staying with them, so he continued to search. It had taken a while, but he finally found a company name associated with Hamilton and the record he was seeking. If she couldn't be at her Uncle Walton's house on the river, then her next favorite spot would be the beach. She had talked often about her childhood days spent at the ocean with her sister and cousins playing in the sand. A quick search of the area map online convinced him this was the address he was seeking.

Once Zane had located the house, he parked where she couldn't see him, but he could keep an eye on her. It had been fortuitous she had picked that precise moment to call him on her cellphone and he'd not only talked to her, but picked up the call on his listening device in the back of the truck. He knew then, without a shadow of a doubt, she was in that house. It was also lucky for him she had decided to go out on an errand

and he'd caught a glimpse of her. He had been worried she had changed her hair or done something to disguise herself out of her fear of James, but she looked as radiant and beautiful as ever in her purple shirt and body-hugging jeans. It had been difficult for him to be so close to her and not rush to her. It would happen in its own time he knew.

He was grateful his mother had taught him the gift of patience. They had experienced it together as they waited for a foal to be born. He would check and find the mare's teats waxed over and her bag getting full, and he would beg his mother to let him do the night watch. She would tell him "Soon enough, Zane. Soon enough." He would watch her as she made those eyes at Iron Crow, and Iron Crow would smile back at her, winking as if they had some huge secret. Now he understood the secrets they had kept. A foal would be coming, and the two of them would be on time to wake him, and get him out to the barn. Some nights it would be so cold the foal would be steaming when its mother pushed it out onto the straw.

Until now, it had never occurred to Zane that most of those nights those two had been wrapped in a single blanket, watching him as he entered the stall and his little hands touched a foal for the first time. His hands were the first human hands those horses felt. He would imprint himself on them, so it was no wonder when he went out into the herds that some of them would come to greet him, seeking out those hands again. Even now, although long years had passed, the horses came to him. Most of those he'd imprinted had passed, yet the new ones seemed to know him. He shook his head as a chill ran up his spine, remembering these subtle things he'd truly missed.

For now, Zane had to use his patience and understanding to guard the most priceless filly of them all. He loved this woman beyond anything he had ever felt, and now he was so close to her. He settled himself into the truck seat for what would feel like a long night.

CHAPTER 16

"Hello?"

The voice on the other end sounded confused and surprised.

"Sorry. Did I wake you? It's Catherine."

"Catherine, hi. I must have overslept," said Celia, sitting up in bed and pushing off the covers. "Olivia's at her grandmother's house for a sleep over, and I had no reason to wake up, I suppose." Celia cleared her dry, raspy throat as she reached for her robe.

"Do you want to call me back?" Catherine asked.

"Could I? That would be lovely. Give me a few minutes, will you?"

"Of course. I'll talk to you soon."

Five minutes later, Catherine's cellphone rang.

"That was quick," Catherine said. There was silence on the phone. "Hello. Is anyone there?" It made Catherine feel sick to her stomach. She hurriedly disconnected the call. The dead space on the phone hadn't happened since right before James showed up at the farm. Two minutes later, the phone rang again. Catherine waited until the third ring and answered it.

"Catherine, hi; it's Celia. I tried to call you a few minutes ago, but there was something wrong with your phone."

"Oh, thank God it was you. It scared me."

"I'm sorry. Are you okay?"

"Yes, I'm fine now. I'm a bit spooked, I guess." She pushed her hair behind her ear and sighed.

"Well, I can certainly understand why. Did anything else happen?"

"No, not really. I thought this little white truck was following me yesterday, but I guess I was imagining things."

"You can't be too careful, though."

"I know, but I don't want to be ridiculous either. I talked to Zane by the way."

"Oh, you say that so casually. By the way, huh? How did it go?"

"I'm not sure. I got defensive. He wanted to come get me. In a way, I wanted him to, and yet I'm not sure I'm ready."

"When do you think you will be?"

"I haven't a clue. I still have this twinge of not trusting him."

"Who or what can you trust these days, honestly, Catherine? There aren't any guarantees with anything. We kid ourselves if we think we know what's going to happen. I can't say I don't plan ahead and hope for the best, but what if what we are living isn't real? I mean I recently found out *Finding Nemo* is about the five stages of grief. Seriously? I thought it was about a handicapped fish."

Catherine started laughing uncontrollably.

"Okay, do you want to tell me what's so funny?"

"Oh, Celia. You are. You are a breath of fresh air," Catherine said, sitting on the arm of the sofa. "I'm so damn serious, but somehow you relate everything to the ocean and make it simple. I love that movie, and now since you mention it, I realize Nemo did have a disability. I never thought about him being crippled by his fin." She laughed again, and tears began to roll down her cheeks.

Celia couldn't help but laugh herself as Catherine's giggle was contagious.

"It's kind of silly, isn't it? Here you two are wasting so much time worrying about what happened yesterday when you could just keep swimming."

Catherine grabbed a few tissues from the box on the kitchen counter.

Scared Truths

"Can you hold on for a minute?"

"Sure."

"Sorry," she told Celia. "I had to blow my nose and dry my tears. Remember I told you I have been having these dreams where I'm swimming, swimming, swimming, and in one of those dreams, I feel like I'm drowning. In another, I'm being pushed by a dolphin. Now, you're telling me we should just keep swimming. It's funny how it all ties to water. It reminds me of the time after Uncle Walton died and an otter came up at the dock."

"That was wonderful, you know."

"Yes, it was. I spent so much time as a child at the river and ocean, and now I'm able to be here at the beach house and spend time with you. It's as if we were meant to meet this way and I was meant to have Zane in my life. Why else would he break down right near my farm? He even has his beautiful Arabian stallion and I have Arabian mares. It's bizarre, don't you think?"

"Bizarre and slightly magical too, right? You do know otter medicine is about women's healing and recovery—otters are sea dogs and playful. They remind us life is to be full of joy."

"How do you stay so positive? You always see the bright side." Catherine ran her finger over the night stand and wiped the dust on her nightgown.

"It's a decision," Celia said, becoming serious. "I learned it a long time ago from this French gentleman I met. I swore we must have been lovers in another life. It was as if he could see into my soul. He became a dear friend and confidant. He taught me a lot about life."

"Your mentor—your soul mate?"

"Yes, indeed. So, let me ask you this: Are you beginning to realize where you are headed?"

"I am. He told me he loves me again."

"And?"

"I told him I needed some time," said Catherine, feeling deflated.

"Do I need to come slap you upside your head?" Celia laughed. "Catherine, nothing lasts forever. What are you waiting for?"

"I wish I knew."

"Time is the indefinite continuation of the progress of your existence."

"What?" asked Catherine, nearly laughing at her sister's astuteness.

"Time is indefinite. It is the continuation of your progress. Of your existence. You can stop or start the progression. You have to decide if you want to exist alone or with a partner."

"There you go again, making it sound easy." Catherine stood and stared out the second-floor window at the ocean. It was the deepest turquoise she had ever seen.

"I didn't get this way without a lot of work, a lot of studying, and a lot of decision making. It gets easier when you accept the Law of Allowance."

"Is this what some people call psychobabble?"

"Maybe, but it really does work. It has helped me a lot. It is the law that basically allows the desired experience to manifest through thoughts, words, and deeds. So, if you wanted to have the perfect partner, you may have manifested Zane to show up in your life."

"Do you really believe that?"

"It doesn't mean you won't have some bumps in the road, but my life has pretty much manifested itself the way I pictured it. Lovely house, wonderful man, beautiful daughter, and loving grandmother."

"Yes, you do seem to have it together," Catherine admitted, pacing in front of the window.

"This house has quite a story. It belonged to a couple we knew. They were elderly and this was their dream home. They had it built the year they both turned eighty. They only lived in it three years when he died. She soon grew ill and had to go into a nursing home. My husband and I met them when he was helping them furnish the house. They fell in love with Olivia."

"Who wouldn't? She's delightful."

"Thank you. They had no living family. It was a shock when their attorney contacted us to tell us they had left the house to us. Can you imagine?"

"No, I can't, but how wonderful for you. I have goose bumps," Catherine stared out at the ocean, feeling glad such a miracle had happened for Celia.

"My husband, Cary, helped pick out the furniture, and now he gets to live here and enjoy it. We thought it would be hard on Olivia, you know, losing them so soon, but she knows how much they loved her, and it brings her immense joy to be loving their house for them. Who knew?

"So, is this another example of the fate thing?" Catherine asked.

"Well, yes, and there's something else. We sold the house Mimi helped us buy to a struggling young couple. Their dream came true too."

"What a sweet story."

"So let me ask you again: How much time is it going to take for you to make this decision?"

"I'm giving myself until the end of the week."

"Okay then. It's a start."

"It's better than yesterday."

"Yes, it certainly is," Celia confirmed. "I'll talk to you soon. Love you."

"Love you right back, and yes, I am quite aware that not so long ago, we didn't even know we were related. I suppose it's part of this scheme too."

"I really believe it is," Celia agreed. "Bye."

Catherine sighed as she hung up the phone, pointing a finger toward the ceiling as she whispered, "Thank you, God."

~~~~~

Zane had parked the truck somewhat hidden across the road from Catherine's driveway. He was startled by someone tapping on his window. He pushed the button and rolled down the dark glass. A deputy in a forest green uniform was peering in at him.

"I had a complaint about a suspicious vehicle. Are you Zane Wheeler?"

"Yes, sir."

"I ran a check on the truck tag. I'll need to see your identification and registration."

"I can be on my way, officer. I was dozing off driving, so I pulled over."

"Nice try, but I'll still need your info, sir."

Zane pulled his license and paperwork out of the console and reluctantly handed them to the officer.

"You'll find this in order. I might as well tell you. I have this place under surveillance."

"Sure thing. I'll be back in a minute."

It didn't take long for the officer to return and tell Zane to at least get the truck farther off the road next time.

"You really are not allowed to park here, but you've been given some sort of special clearance, sir."

"No problem."

As the deputy pulled away, Zane spotted Catherine's vehicle pulling out of her drive. It was a damn good thing the cop had woke him. He would have to drink more damn coffee or something. He gave her a bit of a lead and pulled onto the roadway, following her to Jensen Beach Boulevard. He watched as she pulled into the grocery store. He did a U-turn and parked farther away from her this time.

~~~~~

Catherine made her way into the store, grabbed a cart, and stood where she could see out. She scanned the parking lot. She had a sick feeling something wasn't right. It didn't take her long to spot the pickup truck parked not too far from her car. She pulled out her cellphone and called Celia.

"Are you doing anything important?"

"Not really. Olivia is at camp with her friend today. Mimi dropped her off."

"Is it possible for you to come to the grocery store down the road from your house and meet me inside? I want you to check something out with me. What are you wearing?"

"Why? What do you want me to wear?"

"Do you happen to have a turquoise shirt and a plain pair of jeans?"

"Sure."

"Then wear those. I'll explain when you get here. And wear your hair down."

Catherine waited impatiently in the front of the store, watching the white pickup and waiting for Celia. She was relieved when Celia joined her after about fifteen minutes.

"See the white pickup with the darkly tinted windows?" she said, pulling Celia toward the store's front window far enough away from the earshot of the cashiers. "Well, I swear it's the same truck that followed me to the bookstore yesterday."

"Oh, no!"

"Yes, and a cop was checking it out when I pulled out of my drive to come over here today."

"Are you serious?"

"I'm not as scared as I was now that I'm getting angry. I thought about calling the cops, but now I want to do this myself. I have an inkling I know who this is."

"Don't you think it's kind of dangerous?"

"I have mixed feelings. I really don't think James would be tailing me. I would, however, expect him to confront me again. He's bold, but I have to say, somewhat stupid. However, I wouldn't put this past Zane or one of his cohorts. This seems to be what they would do."

"Still," said Celia, "I don't know if I would tackle this myself. It's one thing to be brave, but, like you said, quite another to be stupid."

"Will you hear me out?" Catherine asked.

"Okay."

"In case you haven't noticed, we do look quite a bit alike. We certainly are related when it comes to the gene pool. What if you pretend to be me and go out and get in my vehicle? If you keep your head down, I don't think whoever is in the truck will realize you are not me."

"Okay? Then what?"

"So, you go get in my car. When I call you on your cellphone, you can get out and start looking under the car or something. Keep your back to the pickup and act like there is something you are absolutely upset about. Flap your arms, you know. Keep bending down looking under the car. Meanwhile, I'm going to circle around and see if whoever is in the truck reacts to your dilemma at all. I really don't think we will be in any danger, and we will do this together. You'll be on your cellphone and they won't know who you are talking to. Want to try it?"

"I guess so. Are you sure we'll be safe?"

"We are in a public parking lot with lots of traffic in and out. I think we'll be fine."

"Okay then. Exactly where is your car?"

Catherine pointed out the window and directed Celia.

"Look at my keys. If anything happens, push the alarm button and set the damn thing off, okay?"

"Got it."

Catherine watched as Celia headed toward her car. She kept her head down, looking at her feet, and turned and got in. Catherine dialed Celia's number on her cellphone and Celia answered.

"Hopefully, whoever this is will be focused on you," said Catherine. "I'm coming out of the store and circling around. As soon as you see me heading toward the white truck, get out of the car, okay?"

"Okay," said Celia.

Catherine took a deep breath. "Here we go."

Scared Truths

Zane was watching Catherine like a hawk as she walked out of the store and toward her vehicle. He started up the truck so that as soon as she pulled out, he could tail her again. He was baffled since she had been in the grocery store for over thirty minutes, but came out empty-handed. He couldn't figure out what she had been doing in there all that time. He watched her get inside her car and waited for it to start moving. Instead, the driver's door suddenly opened and she got out again. The next thing he knew she was looking under her car and waving her arms. It startled him. She looked under her car again while talking on her cellphone. It looked like something was seriously wrong. He opened his truck door and got out.

"Okay, I've got him," someone yelled from behind him.

Zane was staring straight at who he thought was Catherine when she turned and looked in his direction. Something didn't seem right as he turned to face the voice he'd heard. Catherine was staring right at him with a cellphone up to her ear.

"Catherine!" Zane gasped.

"Hell, no, I'm not okay," Catherine said as she pushed the button on her phone.

She started yelling at Zane. "You came here stalking me? You followed me to Florida? I told you to stay away," she said as she stuck her phone in her back pocket.

"I was worried sick about you," he protested. "Yes, I came looking for you. And who is she anyway?" he asked as he turned toward the woman walking up to them.

"I'm her sister, Celia," she replied, "and I'm glad it was you in the truck and not someone else. This scared me half to death."

"You two were pretty damn stupid to do this. What if it wasn't me?"

"I had an inkling it was you," Catherine said. "I guess I should be grateful you taught me a little bit about surveillance, Zane."

"I guess you can say it backfired on me." He tried to laugh.

"Don't laugh. It isn't funny."

"Well, I think I will exit and let you two figure all this out," Celia said. "If it's okay with you, Catherine?"

"I'll be fine. I'm okay now. Thank you." She hugged her. "I'll call you later," she said as Celia handed her the car keys. "I want to see Olivia. Okay?"

"Yes, definitely. Call me. And nice to meet you, Zane."

Catherine spun around and started walking toward her car.

"Where are you going?" Zane asked.

"Away from you."

Zane bolted after her and grabbed her arm.

"I've only been here since yesterday. I checked into a place called the Seaglass Motel over on Indian River Drive."

Catherine laughed. "Ironic. You were right near the cottage we lived in when we moved here from Pennsylvania."

"It's a nice little place. I didn't leave anything in the room, though, so I can call them and check out if you like. They can bill my credit card."

"Oh, so you think you can appear and then step right back into my life?"

"I don't know what you want, Catherine."

"I know."

The silence was deafening as she leaned back against her car and folded her arms.

"Don't push it," she finally said.

"I won't. I want us to be together. I want to help you figure it out. I want you to feel safe. Can we go someplace and talk?"

She sighed and uncrossed her arms.

"Okay, but this is only to talk. Understand? Since you already know where it is, let's go to the beach house."

Catherine ducked into her Lincoln. Zane walked the short distance and got into his truck. It didn't take them long to arrive back at the house. He grabbed the only bag he really needed and quietly followed her through the garage and into the house as the garage door closed.

"Make yourself at home while I turn on a few lights," Catherine said.

"Sure, it's a beautiful place."

"Belongs to my mother and stepfather. It's been a nice get-a-way for me. Plus, I don't think James ever knew about it; why I felt safe until now. How exactly did you find me?"

"Ran a check of the county tax records for property owned by your parents. It took a little digging."

"This is the part of technology I hate. I guess James could have found me too then. Nothing is sacred anymore."

"It wasn't so easy, but I know what you mean. There are no sacred truths."

"I don't know what you mean. Sacred truths? You mean no lies?"

"A sacred truth is a holy truth, the truest form of reality."

"Truest reality? How do you come up with this stuff? Do you mean we have to define reality? My reality certainly changed rather abruptly, didn't it?"

"It did, but it doesn't mean you can't have a better reality now."

"I scrutinized every aspect of what happened, and I doubted every single decision James made, not to mention my own decisions. Then I discovered how much I should have scrutinized you and Buck. That was my reality, wasn't it?"

Catherine was standing in the middle of the kitchen with her hands on her hips.

"You can't take responsibility for or carry anything James did," said Zane, cautiously approaching her. "You can only be responsible for your own decisions, and there really wasn't any right or wrong. You couldn't have known. As for Buck and me, we were just looking out for you."

"You keep telling me that. Then why did it feel so awful? I felt totally betrayed by all of you." Catherine shrugged her shoulders and sank into a chair.

"You were in shock. You were raw and vulnerable and I didn't think you were ready to handle the truth. Not in its entirety. That's why I tried to protect you."

"You fed me bits and pieces instead of telling me the truth?"

"No, I wasn't doing that!" he said emphatically. "You were making your own discoveries. I was simply trying to keep you from hurting so much. It seemed like everyone you loved ended up hurting you, and I didn't want to do that to you."

"You're right, you know. I do realize you tried to protect me. He didn't. James made his decisions without thinking through the consequences and their effect on us—on me. It was his immaturity I suppose. His lack of family affected him in a way. He never thought beyond himself, really."

"That was his reality then?" Zane was standing over her.

"Yes, I think it was. At any rate, I couldn't go back. Knowing what I know now, I wouldn't want to. Seeing him like that. What he did to me and to Arianne as well—he hurt her too. She even tried to protect me. Do I appear so weak everyone feels compelled to save me?"

"Not at all. I think you draw people to you because you are strong and a phenomenal person. Maybe she wished she could be you. Besides, James loved you. He must have because he wanted so much for you, and he made sure you were taken care of even when he knew he failed."

"I never looked at it that way."

"People do the best they can at any given moment. Don't you think he would go back and apply for a do over if he could? Wouldn't Roger?"

"Oh, God. I don't even want to go there. Roger? Okay, okay. I've had enough of this, this delving into the past. I guess we need to answer the question about us. Where do we go from here? Is there even anything left of us? What is that reality?"

"How can you even ask? We are here together right now. I love you. I love you. Can you hear me?"

He watched as she began to shake.

"I want to believe you, Zane."

"Then do. Let's make this our sacred truth. That we will hold that for each other. No lies. No deceit. No doubt. Only truth."

"How can you promise me?"

Scared Truths

"How can you? It's simple. We tell each other everything."
"Everything?"

CHAPTER 17

There wasn't any way Roger could tell how long he had been there. He felt like his mind was playing tricks on him. He wasn't in any pain, he didn't appear to have any injuries, and yet he was in some sort of hospital. He didn't know exactly what happened to him, but people seemed to be trying to help him. He felt a sort of strange euphoria since he didn't have any responsibilities, except allowing them to feed and bathe him, and to cooperate with those who were working hard to get him to speak and walk. He couldn't say a word, but recently, things people said to him had begun to make some sense.

He had also begun to have dreams. In the beginning, they appeared in short segments. He saw a room in black and white, small, sparsely furnished. During one sequence, he saw a city with tall buildings. He could only see the tops of the buildings outside the window from where he was, but they seemed slightly familiar, like the ones in his dream. He didn't know how he could know certain things while other things evaded him.

The door opened suddenly and a tall blonde nurse appeared. "Good morning, Mr. Halvesord. I'm Nancy. I'm here to work with you on speech today. How are you feeling?"

Roger simply stared at her, unable to respond. He could pick up his arms now, so he tapped on the metal bed table once.

"I see. I'm assuming that means good. Let's try this. Tap once for yes and twice for no. So, let's assume you are telling me you are good. Since you have use of your arms, has anyone given you an opportunity to write?"

Roger didn't respond because he didn't know what she meant. He tried to look at her with a questioning face, but he didn't even know if his face moved.

"Well then, let's see what we can do."

Nancy pulled a chair up alongside the bed. She pulled a clipboard from her bag along with a large black felt pen. She said, "Rightie or leftie? Do you know what that means?"

Roger lifted his right hand and Nancy placed the large pen in his fingers.

"Okay, are you able to write your name? Do you know who you are?"

Roger attempted to make the pen mark on the paper, but it slid across the page uncontrollably.

"It's okay. It's a start. Let me help you."

Nancy held Roger's hand. Slowly and patiently, she assisted him in writing his name.

"We will start right here today. I bet in no time all of this will make sense again. We are starting over. Do you understand? We have to teach you everything over again. You had a stroke. Did they tell you? Your brain had an injury, and now we have to re-teach the part of the brain that's been damaged. Do you understand what I am telling you? Yes, or no? One tap for yes and two taps for no."

Roger let go of her hand and tapped the clipboard once.

"I'm excited for you. This is a big step from where you were when you were admitted. Think of this as a portal, and you are getting a second chance at life. We simply have to get you through this portal. Okay?"

Roger tapped again once and tried to smile at Nancy. She pulled a tissue from the box next to his bed and wiped saliva from his chin.

"I'm really proud of you. We'll do this together. I'll be back tomorrow. You'll see. You can do this."

She patted his hand and smiled as she left his room.

Roger let himself relax into his pillow. At least he knew now what had happened. He knew the word stroke meant something to him. He had to figure out what.

~~~~~

Down the hall, an angry James Campbell was fighting the restraints holding him to his bed. He wanted out of this place, and he wanted out now. A nurse had been dispatched by Dr. Finley to give him a mild sedative. They didn't want him knocked out; they needed him to be cooperative.

"It's hard to tell if he's angry as a result of the near drowning and brain injury, or if he's a disagreeable patient," the nurse told Dr. Finley.

"Well, let's assume it's part of his recovery and see if we can't get it under control."

Dr. Finley made his way down the hall to Roger Halvesord's room. He would give the medication time to work before he went to see James.

"Well, Roger, I'm hearing encouraging things about you. We seem to be making some progress. We are optimistic you will, at the least, learn to communicate with us through writing soon. Keep up the great work. We are going to start sending you downstairs to the rehab center tomorrow. I think it will do you a world of good to get out of this bed and your room for a little while."

Roger was trying to comprehend what the doctor was saying, but he couldn't keep up with stringing the words together so they made any sense.

"I'll check on you tomorrow," Dr. Finley said as he made his way out into the hall.

He ran into Jessica.

"Has the medication made any changes in James' attitude yet?" he asked her.

"A little. He's not fighting the restraints, but he's still a bit loud."

"Well, let me see what I can do with him."

Jessica nodded as she headed down the hall. Dr. Finley slowly opened James' door and entered the dimly lit room. He suspected the nurses had closed the blinds to try to subdue the patient. James was glaring at him.

"Get me the hell out of wherever the hell I am! Why do you have me tied down like a damn dog?" he shouted.

"Good morning, James. I see you're a little agitated today. Let's see what we can do here."

"You damn well better do something."

"I know you are upset, but I'm ecstatic now that you seem to have full use of your vocabulary. I do need to inform you that you've suffered a partial brain injury, and although you feel like you are in control, your body may not be functioning as well as you think."

"Let me the hell out of here and I'll show you, you stupid son of a bitch."

"Well now, if you want me to continue to be your physician, you will have to behave respectfully toward me."

"Respect. If you had any respect for me, you would undo these damn handcuffs."

"Restraints, restraints, James. They are to keep you safe. You've been a bit out of control. I ordered a medication to calm you down. Let me get a nurse in here."

Dr. Finley stuck his head out the door and spotted one of the younger nurses. He called out to her and asked her to come help him. He told her to stay on the other side of the bed in case James needed her assistance. Dr. Finley unbuckled the left ankle restraint, then the left arm restraint. He motioned for the nurse to unbuckle the two restraints.

"Well, there you go, Mr. Campbell. I've released you."

James tried to sit up, but he couldn't get his arms underneath him to push himself up. He tried rolling on his side, but he was too weak. Nothing he did would allow him to get out of the bed. He couldn't even sit up on his own.

"You've been in a coma, Mr. Campbell. You have had a brain injury, which is interrupting messages to parts of your body. You have been bed bound for quite some time, and you have to allow yourself to heal. Instead of using your energy to fight with the restraints and the staff, you might want to consider utilizing your energy for the greater good, which would mean your recovery."

"I can do this; give me a minute. I'll get out of here," he said angrily.

James tried again to sit up, but all he could do was lift his body away from the pillow for a few seconds. He fell back and sighed.

"Okay, Doc. I guess you win this one."

"I will make you a deal," said Dr. Finley. "You stop fighting with us and I'll get you out of this room for a bit every day. I'll write an order to send you down to rehab starting tomorrow. That should make a significant change in your recovery, as well as your attitude. However, you have to work at it. Deal?"

"Okay, Doc. I'll do it, but don't let them tie me up."

"Don't make it necessary to restrain you, and they won't."

~~~~~

In the morning, as promised, two male nurses moved James carefully to a wheelchair and he was taken by elevator downstairs. The first glimpse James Campbell had of anyone else in the rehab area sent him into a tailspin. The guy right smack in front of him looked a great deal like his old buddy, Roger Halvesord, but how could it be him? He knew he had given him a fatal dose in the drink he'd fixed him. Roger should have been dead as a doornail. Maybe his mind was playing tricks on him. He kept staring at the man in the wheelchair across from him. The guy was really thin and emaciated, with ghastly white skin, but he sure resembled his former friend.

"Now, James, you need to focus on the task at hand. We will take this one step at a time. Dr. Finley has high hopes you will be cooperative today. Right?"

James had been stuck in bed long enough. He was motivated to get out of there.

"Right, right. Let's get this damn show on the road." He tried to push himself up out of the wheelchair and stand. The therapist grabbed him right before he began to reel forward and pushed him back into a sitting position in his wheelchair.

"Hey, buddy, you can't do that. You have to gain your strength back a little bit at a time. You've been stuck in bed for a while. Your muscles need to be awakened, and it's going to take some work. Plus, you can't take me out with you." He laughed out loud.

"I don't have time to sit in this damn chair. I want to get out of this place. I don't want to look like him."

James pointed at the man he thought looked like Roger.

"Now, now, we don't do things like that either. All of you have your issues. You can't compare yourself to others."

"Who is he, anyway? He looks vaguely familiar."

"We aren't allowed to discuss other patients. Only first names are given. His name is Roger. I can't tell you anything else."

James nearly gasped, because it was not what he wanted to hear. Surely it wasn't, couldn't be, Roger Halvesord, his old college roommate and attorney.

"He really does look familiar. Is he from here?"

"I can't discuss other patients with you, Mr. Campbell. I've already told you, but I do believe he's a resident of New York."

James nearly banged his arm on his wheelchair, but he caught himself. The son of a bitch had lived. Now what the hell was he going to do?

"He looks like he's in pretty bad shape. Can he talk?"

"Mr. Campbell, let's focus on getting you out of this chair, okay? Each person in here has their own priorities. We are here to help you get well. Let's focus on getting you walking again."

James shook his head. What the hell were the chances of this?

"Am I in New York?" he asked.

"Yes. Didn't they tell you? You are in New York City at one of the finest brain injury rehab centers in the country."

"No, I didn't know. Today's the first time I've been out of my room."

"Well, then, let's get started."

All James wanted to do was get well and get the hell out of there before his old buddy started talking. So far, he didn't think Roger had even noticed him. He couldn't help but wonder why the damn dosage hadn't worked.

CHAPTER 18

The sun warmed Catherine's face as she stretched and pulled the covers over her head. She couldn't believe she was waking up in Jensen Beach and Zane was right across the hall. It seemed ridiculous. They had talked late into the night. Her whole life suddenly felt unreal again. Was she dreaming? One thing was certain; she felt ready to make a decision, and she knew it was the right one.

She could smell coffee and bacon as she pulled the covers off her face and rolled out of bed. She slipped out of her nightgown and ran to the bathroom completely naked. She would never get used to the lack of privacy. The bedroom window faced the ocean and was completely without any curtains or anything.

"I can hear you running around up there. How long before you come down?" called Zane.

"Give me five minutes. Okay?"

"Scrambled or over easy?"

"Scrambled is fine."

She smiled at herself in the mirror. What a difference a day made. Was she really ready to go back with Zane? *So much for waiting for the end of the week*, she thought as she brushed her teeth and clipped up her hair. Catherine jumped in the shower as soon as the water was warm. She rinsed off and grabbed one of the fluffy towels, wrapped herself in it, and scooted across the master bedroom to the walk-in and her suitcase. She grabbed a long loose shirt and a clean pair of jeans, let down her hair and re-clipped it in place as she hurried down the stairs.

Zane was at the stove pouring scrambled eggs into a skillet.

"I still can't believe you are here. How did this happen? It feels like a dream. Us ending up here together in my old hometown."

"We love each other. It's simple. Love prevails," he said.

"Do you truly believe that?"

"Much more right at this moment than ever before in my life."

"Good," she said and squeezed his arm, holding back from hugging him.

"Catherine, you have no idea how much I wanted this day. I hope you're hungry. Let's have breakfast, and then I have a lot to share with you."

"I'm starving."

It had been weeks since she'd felt hungry and she was also excited because she had something she wanted to tell Zane.

~~~~~

They had their breakfast outside on the patio, listening to the sound of the early morning waves and the call of a few seagulls. The ocean was crystal clear and a rich, deep turquoise. The sea grapes and tall grasses swayed slightly in the morning breeze. It certainly seemed like paradise. Zane reached across the table and took her hand in his.

"Catherine, I know this has been a difficult time for you, but you have truly been strong in how you've handled it. A lot happened in a short period of time, including my coming into your life. Some of it would have brought most people to their knees. You've done remarkably well."

She didn't say a word, but sat tentatively waiting to see where he was heading.

"I don't want to erase the times we had together, but I would like to make a deeper commitment to you starting from here. I will fill in any areas you have questions about any time you want to ask. There will be no secrets. Like I said, I have a lot to tell you. Most people have secrets they have kept or lies they tell. Some are unintended lies used to protect people. Sometimes those lies lead people into lives they never dreamed of, sort of like what accidentally happened with us."

Catherine sighed and said, "I know, Zane. I understand you and Buck were trying to protect me. I understand James thought he was protecting me. I read the report Roger sent me, so I know the lies, intended or not, weren't put in place to hurt me. It still doesn't help me forgive James for not trusting me. It still gives me pause not to trust you."

"I get it. Truly I do, but I am telling you right now, I will honor our relationship by keeping it sacred, and telling you the truth. Here's what I'm thinking. I happen to know Buck and Deb are in need of a break from their own chaotic lives. Buck wants to take Deb to Montana. I talked to Effie while I was on the road the other day and we concocted a plan. She and Roan will stay at Buck's and take care of the kids for a few days. Roan will cover the feed store since he's been helping Buck there and he knows what to do. Your house will be open, so we can go check on our animals, catch our breath, and then decide what we want to do. How does that sound? Effie and Roan are okay with whatever we want to do."

Catherine hadn't expected this. She thought he would beg her to go to Montana.

"I really have been concerned and missing my animals. I think it would be wonderful to be back at my farm."

"We will also get both our vehicles to the farm. I thought maybe once you see everything is truly okay, then maybe, just maybe, you would consider going to Montana with me to meet my mother and Iron Crow. Would you think about it? You don't have to decide right now."

"I'll need a little time to say goodbye to my parents, my sister, Kiki, and also to go say goodbye to Celia and Olivia. I've barely had any time with Olivia at all."

"Well, if this works out the way I would like it, once we are living back on the farm, you can come down here whenever you want, since I'll be there to care for the animals. It's not like you can't come back."

"Of course. I know that. It's more sudden than I expected. I'm not complaining at all. I only want to see them to say goodbye in person."

"It's fine, Catherine. I will have the rest of my life with you." He smiled at her. "Or at least I hope I do."

She hadn't allowed him to kiss her, and she certainly hadn't let him back in her bed. She stood up and started collecting the dishes, sticking the silverware in a glass.

"I know you're right, Zane. I've been in a sort of shock over everything. It seemed like nothing was clear or true for me."

"When you hear what I have to tell you about my trip to Montana, you will understand how well I know the feeling now."

"What do you mean?" Catherine asked.

"It's incredible to think how sometimes exactly what you want is right there staring you in the face and you don't even know it. You may even have a gut feeling about something, and yet you deny the truth even to yourself."

"But I didn't have any signs about James. At least nothing was apparent. He kept control of everything. It was his behavior with Arianne that's bothering me the most. Now since being with you, I realize it was also the way he treated me. I had no barometer to gauge it before, so I thought the way he treated me was normal. Does that make any sense?"

"Yes, it makes perfect sense."

"He was a master at manipulation. He would tell me he was only teasing with Arianne and it meant nothing. Now I know the truth about how intimate they really were." Catherine sighed and pushed her hair back behind her ears. "The most difficult part is learning it was happening before, during, and after me. It's hard to take."

"I know how much it hurt you, and I don't mean to make this sound like your thinking is skewed, but by the time people reach adulthood, the vast majority of them have had more than one bed partner. Most of them do not allow that to define who they are. I'm guessing you were completely loyal to James."

"Yes, of course I was." She stared at the floor, quietly contemplating her next words. "I came from the mindset of being a good girl until you married."

"And, Catherine, there is nothing wrong with that, but understand it's rare these days. James apparently didn't see his behavior in the same light as you did. At the same time, he was trying to protect you and himself from an upheaval in the marriage. All the while, he was getting what he wanted at your expense."

She placed her hands on her hips and said, "Exactly. Meanwhile, I was constantly second-guessing myself and trying to please him."

"I hope you don't feel the same way with me."

"Well, I was skeptical of you, and when I realized what you had done for me when I was sick, I was embarrassed and it scared me." Catherine stood up from the patio chair and gazed out over the dunes at the ocean.

"I knew it did, but who was going to take care of you?"

She turned to face Zane. "I understand, and I'm grateful. I think my recovery went much faster once I was home and in your loving care. Then, as I got stronger and we got to know each other, you were so charming. I was even skeptical of that part of you. I thought you were playing me."

"What happened to change your mind?"

"It was the way you cared for Trouble, the time you spent with my horses, the way the dogs interacted with you. The clincher was when you told me about how you rescued the kitten and cared for her. The relationship you had with her melted my heart."

"Oh, so if you hadn't had those animals, you would have kicked me to the curb?"

Catherine couldn't resist his broad smile—the way his eyes twinkled.

"No, you were a charmer, for sure. I gave in and went for broke. I never in my life allowed my guard down like that and went on total impulse. I let go of my fear to be with you."

"And?"

"Oh, my God, Zane." She grabbed his shoulders and shook him. He reached up, pulling her into his lap, and kissed her. He was grinning from ear to ear when his lips finally released hers.

"So, does this mean you'll go to your farm and then to Montana with me? You have to meet my mother. You have to. And Parker Iron Crow, of course."

"Yes, yes, yes. If Buck and Deb agree, we will go relieve the Matthews for a few days, and if everything is okay on the farm, we will get on a plane and fly away. Yes, Zane Wheeler, I will go to Montana with you."

She buried her head in the crook of his neck, snuggling into his warmth. It seemed like it had been forever.

~~~~~

Zane helped Catherine carry the dishes through the sliding door and stacked them on the counter. She was busy at the sink when he slid in behind her and began to kiss her neck. When she turned around to face him, he picked her up and headed up the stairs.

"Which room?" he asked.

"It doesn't matter," she whispered.

Curled in each other's arms, staring at the sparkling sea, they made plans to leave Jensen Beach in the morning. In the afternoon, she would make her rounds saying goodbye to Hamilton and her mother. She would ask Kiki to meet her at their house to make it easier. It would be nice for all of them to be together. She couldn't even remember the last time that had happened. Maybe one Christmas when she had come home from college.

She'd go to Celia's house and say goodbye to her and Olivia. She would promise to keep in touch by phone. Then she would say goodbye to her parents and sister.

Scared Truths

After a good night's sleep, she and Zane would drive to Highberry in their separate vehicles. It seemed impossible to think she would be sleeping in her own house the following night. She busied herself cleaning up the beach house and putting things back where she thought they had been. Hamilton told her he would have his housekeeper tidy it up, but she was not going to leave anything out of place.

~~~~~

Zane came in with two bags of ice and headed back out to the truck. When he brought in grocery bags, he said, "I bought some things to make sandwiches and a few snacks for the trip. I'm excited. This will be fun."

"I'm excited, too. I'm leaving in a few minutes to go to Skyline Drive to say goodbye to Celia and Olivia, then say goodbye to Hamilton, my mom, and my sister. They'll be at the Sewall's Point house."

"Do you want me to drive you? I can wait in the truck."

"No, I'll be fine. I honestly don't think James will show up here."

"About that. There's something I need to tell you about James and Roger, Catherine."

Her heart felt heavy in her chest, and she had this sick, sinking feeling in the pit of her stomach. It had come out of nowhere.

"Should I sit down?" She didn't know what to expect.

"You can if you want to."

She did. She sat on a stool at the kitchen island.

"I talked to Buck," Zane said, "and he told me the strangest story. It seems Roger suffered a terrible stroke. Apparently, he was still living in New York, and he's now in a rehab facility there. He can't speak or walk. He's pretty much incapacitated."

"Oh, dear," Catherine said softly. "I mean, I never liked the man, especially after what he tried with me, but no one wants someone to suffer."

"And, that's not all. James was in the Cayman Islands at some resort and they found him nearly drowned on the beach. He was completely naked when they found him."

"My God! That is so strange. Both of them?"

"Well, it gets even stranger. When they searched James' belongings, they discovered he was from New York. You know he's going by James Campbell these days with his new identity and all. He had registered down there as a Mr. James. They also discovered he had quite a bit of cash stashed, and the surprising thing is the authorities didn't make it disappear. Instead, they used part of it to ship him back to the mainland and turned the remainder over to someone in New York. Now get this," Zane said emphasizing the words. "He's in the same rehab as Roger. Can you believe the irony of it?"

Catherine slid off the stool and moved closer to Zane.

"This whole thing seems horrible—unbelievable, really. So, what kind of shape is he in, then? This sounds awful."

"Apparently, James can speak, but he has some kind of brain damage affecting his motor skills. They think it's from the near drowning—probably lack of oxygen."

"I wonder if James and Roger know they are both in the same place."

"I didn't delve into that with Buck. I pretty much only got the basics. I suppose we can get the info when we get to Highberry. The point is you don't have to watch your back anymore. They are both out of commission, at least for the time being."

Catherine walked over to the sliding glass doors and peered out.

"Roger had a stroke—a stroke of all things? And somehow James ends up on an island and nearly drowns." She paused briefly, then continued, "I wouldn't wish this on either of them, but I feel relieved I don't have to be afraid."

"I don't blame you. I wanted to tell you so you can relax a little when you go to see your family and also on this trip. And, of course, no more secrets."

She walked over and put her arms around his neck, peering into his face.

"I honestly have mixed feelings. I don't want them to suffer, but at the same time . . . ."

"Seems karmic to me, huh?"

"I know. It's sad but true."

~~~~~

Catherine didn't waste any time. She told her parents and Kiki she was heading back to Highberry with Zane. The Matthews had to go babysit their grandkids at Buck's, so her house would be hers again. She made it sound like the most exciting news to be going home. She also told them it looked as if she and Zane would be taking a trip to Montana soon, and she would keep them informed. She hugged them each at least twice, telling them she was grateful to have spent even a little bit of time with them. Then she gave Kiki a special squeeze.

"I'm so glad I got to see your ranch," Catherine said. "It's perfect for you. Far enough removed from the hectic world. It's sure not like when we were little girls."

"And isn't it ironic how we both ended up with horses and sort of out in the woods?" Kiki replied.

"I know. It does seem to be all about the animals, doesn't it? If we didn't have them, the ranches wouldn't be necessary."

"I hope," their mother interjected, "you girls appreciate how forgiving I was when those creatures you dragged home ruined something of mine."

They rolled their eyes and laughed.

"Mom," said Kiki, "you were almost as bad as us. You always blamed us, but you were the one who picked them up and put them in the car." Their mom shrugged her shoulders. They all smiled and hugged again.

"It was nice to have you home," Elizabeth said. "You are both reminding me of Nanny. Do you remember the photo of her with the calf and the mule?"

"We loved that picture," Kiki said.

"Well, I found it the other day, and I'm going to get copies made and send one to each of you."

"I would love it, Mom," Catherine said. "It will be perfect on the wall of my sunporch at the farm."

"Be sure and call me with your address, honey," Elizabeth said. "I'm gathering some things I want to send you too. And, Kiki, I have a box in the front hallway for you. Come with me."

"Bye, Mom!" Catherine called to her.

"Let them go," Hamilton said. "I wanted a moment alone with you anyway. Tell me, are you really okay?"

"Yes, thank you. It was quite unexpected, but it has turned out okay after all. In fact, it turned out even better than I had hoped. Some time, I will call you and tell you a tale you will hardly believe."

"Promise?"

"Yes. I promise. I'm so glad I got to see you again. I've come from saying goodbye to Celia and Olivia, too."

"Oh, yes, your mother told me about this long-lost half-sister of yours. I've seen her around town since I learned of the connection, but neither of us has acknowledged the other."

"It's probably just as well. We don't quite know how to handle this with Olivia being so young and me being so far away. Celia and I have kept it kind of low key. There's really no reason to explain to her that I'm her aunt. Maybe someday."

"I understand, and I respect you for it. Seems these days the poor little kids are caught right in the middle of all this family stuff."

"Yes, it does seem unfair, which is why we haven't said anything. Olivia knows we have a lot in common, but beyond that, she only thinks we look alike. For now, it's okay with me."

"Well, please don't keep us in the dark so much. We do worry about you. Your mother simply doesn't know how to express her concern."

"I know. I'll try and do better."

"We can't ask for anything more."

Hamilton hugged her and walked her out the front door. Catherine waved as she got into her vehicle and drove out of the circular drive.

~~~~~

Catherine was grateful it had been an uneventful trip. She drove into her driveway ahead of Zane and had barely gotten out of her vehicle before she could hear the dogs barking. She raced to the door with her key in her hand and slowly unlocked the back porch door.

Zane called to her from the truck to be careful, but it was too late. General launched himself from the doorway, knocking her backwards as Zane came up behind her and caught the two of them. He spun her around and the rest of the dogs surrounded them both. Only little Friskie stood at the top of the steps in the doorway, wiggling all over and barking at them. General took off running large loops all around the yard. Catherine burst into tears of joy.

"Oh, General. Oh, General."

The big dog came bouncing to her and leaped into the air, knocking Catherine down in the grass. In an instant, all of them were on top of her as she covered her face. She was giggling and trying to curl into a ball.

"Okay, okay; that's enough, you guys."

Poor little Friskie had come down a few steps, but he was not about to get into the mix. Zane scooped him up. Once Catherine was standing again, she wiped the grass from her pants and started up the steps into her house. It was amazing to be home.

Everything on the sunporch was right where she had left it. The kitchen seemed to be in order except for the definite smell of something delicious. There was a note on the stove. Mrs. Matthews had left a Crock-Pot full of stew cooking on the counter, and there was a freshly baked apple pie in the oven, safe from the dogs.

"Zane, would you look at this? Mrs. Matthews has cooked us dinner and made us a pie. She's such a thoughtful person."

"Yes, she definitely is."

"I hope the Matthews get a chance to really enjoy those kids these few days."

"I'm sure they will. Meanwhile, I bet we have some hungry dogs here. Isn't this their dinner time?"

"I bet it's why she put the pie back in the oven. One of these scoundrels would have eaten it otherwise."

Zane laughed. "I think there's only one who could have reached it, but I know how generous General would have been."

General hadn't left Catherine's side since she came into the house, and he nuzzled her hand as she stood at the stove. She squatted down, took the big dog's face in her hands, and kissed him.

"Oh, Gen, I've missed you so much. I really did."

"Well, you better take a moment for this little boy." Zane handed Friskie to Catherine.

She had forgotten how adorable he was. She could barely even find his little black eyes in the curly fur on his face. He stuck his little pink tongue out and slowly kissed her nose.

"I know, Frisk; I know. I missed you, too, but I hear you have a great friend in Mr. Matthews. Zane, they all look healthy, and they don't seem distressed. I was so worried, but I had to go."

"Dogs are pretty adaptable. I know there are exceptions, but your guys had each other, and I was pretty sure they'd do okay. They were especially lucky to have Effie and Roan since those two are the greatest when it comes to caring for critters. I have seen them pull quite a few animals from the brink of death. You'd wonder how they could manage it, but at the last minute, the animal would turn around."

"Some people seem to know what to do."

"They have the benefit of generations of cattle people, and most of those people had dogs to work the cows. Those dogs made money for them, so they had better keep them healthy and working. The cows they lost were lost revenue. The dogs earned their keep, and the ranchers kept the dogs well cared for."

"You make it sound like it's all business."

"Oh, no, not with the Matthews. I've been over there on bad nights when they would go out and bring in calves who were half-frozen to death, and everyone would be up all night in the kitchen with those calves trying to pull them through. No, they aren't in it just for the money. They love the lifestyle."

"And what about your ranch? Is it the same?"

"It is now, but I have to tell you, the Wheelers were all about money and controlling their land and cattle holdings. Foster Wheeler was no exception. He pounded into my head how we were wheelwrights and I better appreciate my heritage."

"I know you've mentioned that to me before, but so I'm clear on this, I have to ask. Are wheelwrights the people who made wheels?"

"Yes, and according to Foster Wheeler, the West would have never been conquered without his family's wheels."

"Well, if it's true, that's something to be proud of."

"Yes, but that is a whole other story, and I'd rather save it for a moment when we aren't so tired from driving all day. Can we feed the dogs and ourselves, and I'll share it with you on another day soon?"

"I'm curious, but I'm willing to wait. I'm so delighted to be home, but at the same time, I'm tired. Now, I have to say it. There's no place like home."

Zane kissed her. "You have no idea how happy I am to share this moment with you."

"It sure is a lot different this time driving back from Jensen Beach and falling into your arms." She couldn't stop smiling.

CHAPTER 19

Zane and Catherine hadn't expected Effie to leave them dinner and dessert, but it eliminated a run to the grocery store. The dogs were contently waiting as Zane dished out their food.

"Let's sit out on the porch for a little while before we eat," Catherine said. "I want to take it all in. It seems like forever since we were here, and it's so good to be home."

Zane set the dog bowls at the appropriate places and followed her out to the sunporch. She moved a throw pillow and settled on the love seat. Zane stood in the doorway, looking out across the recently mowed pastures.

"I bet Roan cut it and has it all baled for you for winter. He wouldn't let nice grass go to waste."

"Really? I would have never even thought about doing it. I would have mowed." Catherine stood up for a few seconds to get a better look at the pasture.

"True sign of a rancher. They make every aspect of the ranch work for them, plus you learn to live off the land in rhythm with the seasons. I can't wait to take you home with me."

"I don't know, Zane. It may be hard to pull me away from them again."

"We don't have to stay long. In fact, you can leave whenever you want, and I'll stay on. Now that we know where Roger and James are, I won't be so worried about you."

"I was thinking about it when I was driving. What in the world are the chances of them both ending up like that? Both of them in therapy at the same place?"

"Since you brought it up, do you think it's ironic that Roger had a stroke? Seems like he got a horrible karmic payback."

"Yes, it's a bit surreal to me. Roger's not even the one who came up with the formula. I have read about karmic levels, but a payback? It seems like they both got slammed."

"Don't you think they deserved it?"

"I honestly didn't want to think about them, but they are like my worst enemies. Right when I think my life is okay, they rear their ugliness again. Deserve this? No, not really. It seems awful for them."

"But there were times when I know you felt like they were out to get you, Catherine. I don't think they intended to hurt you the way they did."

"Are you defending them again?"

"Maybe I'm defending their intention. Their initial goal was to protect the country by eliminating some of the bad guys. They simply didn't have the foresight to understand the impact it would have on everyone in their own lives. They didn't think the process through to the end, and I'm not sure anyone in their positions would have."

"I get where you're heading with this. You're trying to make me feel better about who they were, and what they did, but the bottom line will always be they both deceived me."

"Yes, and possibly only because they didn't want you to be a target."

"And yet, in the end, that's exactly what happened. If the government hadn't killed off my James, then I would have likely been a target if the so-called bad guys had found out about the drug. They convinced him to commit a type of pseudocide, didn't they? In the end, I became the target of Roger's desires, and his aspirations certainly included me. He was disgusting to me. I never, ever liked him." Catherine wrapped her arms protectively around herself.

"Wow—pseudocide. Yes. I guess you're right. It was. I know how you feel and why it's almost funny that they are both sitting in rehab in New York trying to recreate their lives."

"I don't think there's anything funny about any part of it. I researched this because it all bothered me so much. Pseudocide is when someone fakes their own death because they want to avoid serious personal problems and start a new life. He thought I would take him back, like he was some kind of hero. He wanted me to simply forgive the lies and deceit."

"Maybe funny is not the right word. Amusing maybe. Let's say it's ironic, since they are almost worse off than the victims the government used their drug on. They are somewhat trapped by their own deceit."

"Okay, okay. Enough of this. Can we forget about them and enjoy the farm? I want to sit here and be peaceful and not have to think about James or Roger ever again."

Zane sat down next to her on the love seat. Friskie jumped, diving onto Catherine's lap while looking up at Zane.

"Yes, I'm sure she missed you too, you little stinker," he said as he petted the little black fur ball.

"I missed everything about this place, Zane. I think you will have a hard time dragging me away." She sighed as she petted Friskie.

"It's only for a little while. You have to come meet my mother and Iron Crow. That's all I ask. My mother is showing signs of slowing down a little, and I don't want to wait until she's not able to share some things with you. I want you to know her. I'm sure you two will have a lot to talk about. In fact, I have some things I want to share with you when we are on our trip."

"You don't want to tell me now?"

"No. I'm going to leave you to your dogs and this fantastic view and head down to the barn to see what Roan has been up to."

"Why don't you say you want to see your horse?" She chuckled.

"Okay, I admit it. I want to see Trouble, and I also want to check out your horses too. Do you want to come?"

"No, I think you're right. I want to savor a little alone time. I'll come down later this evening."

Zane kissed her, got up, and took his gray felt cowboy hat off the hook inside the door, knocking the dust off it on his knee.

"Been missing this."

Catherine smiled up at him and waved him out the door.

~~~~

The days on the farm were going by too fast. Zane knew he would have to push her or the weather would change in Montana. As he walked into the barn, he heard the unmistakable greeting of Trouble. Heads popped up on either side of the aisle, and Sweetie, the barn cat, hurried to him, stopping short when she saw the dogs coming.

"Let her be," he told them. "Take a walk. Go out."

The dogs reluctantly obeyed him, and Sweetie bravely curled herself around his legs. He could hear and feel her purring. When he picked her up, she slid her head up under his chin. He had never expected to be so attached to a cat, but she had been so tiny and frail when he pulled her out of the woodpile. She'd grown into quite the barn cat and often gifted him with mice or worse. He gently placed her back on the ground, and she followed him into the hay room.

Zane loved being in the barn in the early morning. When he walked out with his arms full of hay flakes, every head was turned his way. Once the horses were munching, he dumped all the water buckets and refilled them. He grabbed a broom and swept up the shavings and hay from the barn aisle. He would talk to her at breakfast and set a date to leave for Montana. He couldn't wait to share all the things he loved about the ranch. He was certain, now that Catherine had been home, she would have the confidence to leave again, especially since she knew both James and Roger were incapacitated.

He made his way back toward the house and whistled for the dogs. A couple had already joined him, and he started counting heads. General lagged behind him, but the others were barking and eagerly waiting for him to open the back door. They came onto the porch in a flurry. Catherine leaned toward Zane and kissed him on the cheek.

"Morning."

He took a deep breath, taking in the scent of bacon.

"Oh, you make my heart sing."

"Why?"

"Bacon. You know it's my favorite."

"Mine too. I thought it would be nice to have some and French toast."

"Doesn't get any better."

They ate silently for a few minutes and then he decided to go for it.

"Well, are you about ready for me to take you home to meet my mother and Iron Crow?"

He was trying to read her. She sucked in a big breath and put down her fork.

"About that—you know, I was nervous about leaving my animals before, but I have to say, I think they did really well with the Matthews taking care of them. Normally, I would be protesting, but honestly, I think we should take advantage of their generosity."

He was beyond relieved to hear her say it.

"Oh, Catherine, I can't tell you how happy that makes me. I promise you will love the ranch, and you will love my mother as well. I have so much to share with you. And Iron Crow. Well, let's say he's quite a character."

Zane leaned across the table, took her chin in his hand, and kissed her tenderly.

"You have no idea how glad I am the Matthews are here and I get to take you home for a little while."

"Well, we kind of have a time frame. I talked to Effie, and she said as soon as Buck and Deb get back from their little honeymoon, she and Roan will come over here, but they'd like to be back at their ranch before the weather gets too cold. Do you think two weeks is reasonable for us to be gone?"

Scared Truths

Of course, Zane would have loved to have a month or even longer, but he understood, and he was certain once Catherine saw the ranch, she would want to go back.

"Honey, I would love to keep you there as long as I can, but I do understand about their time frame and yours. I'm so grateful you said yes. We will make it work."

"Well, I'll firm up the dates with the Matthews, and then I'll check out the airlines. Where do you want to fly in to?"

"Great Falls will be fine. We could fly to Kalispell, but you can usually get better flights to Great Falls."

"Okay then."

Zane couldn't believe she had said yes so easily.

"You cooked," Zane said, "so I'll clean up the dishes. Then we can saddle up and take a ride if you like."

"Perfect."

~~~~~

Catherine had tried to pack conservatively. They carried their coats, and Zane was wearing his old weathered hat. It had been a little easier this time for her to say goodbye to all the dogs, knowing they would be safe with the Matthews.

She hadn't flown in a while, and the bustle of the airport and the way they were moved through security was unnerving. She had heeded Zane's warning and worn a comfortable outfit, and her boots had a zipper in the front so she didn't have to untie them. He had also insisted they could afford to sit in first class. She was relieved to have some time in the airport lounge away from all the people, traffic, and noise. Plus, boarding the plane early and having plenty of space in the overhead let her nerves settle down before takeoff.

She couldn't help it. She always felt edgy until the plane was off the runway. Zane hadn't protested at all when she asked for the window seat. It gave her a sense of peace to look out and see land or at least clouds.

"I guess the kids were happy to have Buck and Deb home," said Catherine, once they were buckled into their seats on the plane.

"Buck said he and Deb were sure happy to see them, too. He said they would back up his parents as far as your farm and not to worry."

"It is pretty mind-boggling how all of us found our way to each other. I was thinking about it when we were riding. It's strange how even though parts of this were somewhat prearranged, the main thing is we all ended up in the right place at the right time."

"Serendipitous."

Catherine giggled. "That word sounds funny when you say it. It doesn't seem like something a cowboy would say."

"I read this little book when I was young about three princes who were sent on a journey by their father. The reason they went didn't matter as much to their father as what they learned on the way. It's what happened to Buck and me. He came here to get away from his past, but it followed him. I came here to run from mine, but it caught up with me here."

"I know the story about the princes," Catherine said. "It's been told in several different ways in different cultures. It is strange how we did accidentally end up in relationships. And I would have never put Buck and Deb together. In fact, I thought he really disliked her in the beginning. But then they kind of transformed each other."

"She had her own secrets too. I don't even know if I should tell you this."

The pilot said they would be taking off in a few minutes and the flight was not expected to have any delays.

"What were you saying about Deb?" Catherine asked.

"I was saying I probably shouldn't even tell you this, but I don't want to drag any baggage with me. She was attached to your story as well. She was here watching your situation and Buck's, only on a much lower level. She wanted to get out of the NSA, and this was her way of integrating back into society without drawing any attention to herself."

"What do you mean? Then she wasn't really a real estate agent? Are you kidding?"

"Oh, no. She studied and took the test and was a bona fide realtor. She had attributes you weren't aware of." He laughed.

"Was Buck in on that too? Did he know?"

"As far as I know, Buck found out later, after he was involved with her. Bill, one of our former colleagues, came and told him. I'm not sure if Deb knows Buck knows, though."

"You're saying there are still secrets with you two?"

"I honestly haven't discussed it with him, but she's never said anything to me and we have this code of ethics that some things are best left alone."

"I don't believe it! Will this ever end? Is there anything else?"

The plane began to taxi down the runway. Zane didn't say another thing until they had taken off and leveled out.

"I do want to share with you what I discovered while I was in Montana, but let's enjoy this first part of our trip for now."

He took Catherine's hand in his and held it gently.

"I promise you won't regret coming to the ranch with me. Trust me."

"That's probably not the thing to say, Zane. Trust is something I've had a bit of trouble with lately." She grinned at him.

CHAPTER 20

The plane had leveled out, and the flight attendants were serving drinks. Zane waited until they moved the cart farther down the aisle.

"I've been wanting to tell you about my trip to Montana," he said, "and now, since you're a captive audience, I guess it's as good a time as any."

Catherine turned and smiled at him. "I'm not sure if I'm ready for this since you've been saving it up. I wondered why you hadn't said too much about it at the house. I guess I'm about to find out."

"I think part of my holding back was my own processing. I had a lot going on in my head, and I needed time to sort it out."

"You are kind of scaring me," Catherine said.

"Oh, it has a happy ending. It wasn't a bad journey, but it was different than what I had expected."

"Boy, do I know about expectations. I should have listened to the old adage—no expectations, no disappointments."

"Well, here goes." Zane turned toward Catherine and took her hand. "You know the main reason I wanted to go was to make amends with my mother for taking off the way I did right out of high school. I know it broke her heart. On top of that, I stayed away much longer than I should have. I would call her on special days—her birthday, Christmas—you know. Even when Foster died, I should have gone home for her, but I didn't. I made excuses. I said I was too busy. In reality, I had

Scared Truths

a lot of comp time I could have used. There truthfully was no good reason. I was being selfish."

"Are you sure you want to do this? I mean, do you want to get all worked up about this?"

"I need to tell you. Really, I'm fine."

"Okay, then."

"The minute the plane landed and I left the airport and started driving north, my mind began pulling up old stuff. I rolled down the windows and the scent of the sweet grasses and the sound of the wind sent my mind whirling further and further back. It was very surreal. I was in such a state of deep thought, I almost drove past our road to the ranch. I can't begin to tell you how it felt to be in that familiar area and see those old familiar places. I felt like I was the same young boy who had taken off long ago."

"I can't even imagine."

"I hadn't told my mother I was coming, but she had seen the dust trail from the truck as I came across the flatland headed toward the main gate to the house. She was standing on the front porch when I pulled up. Oh, my God, Catherine. She had on her apron and she was holding the end of it up in her hands the same as when I was a little boy coming home from a long hard ride."

He sipped his drink and took a deep breath.

"I barely got the truck stopped before I jumped out and ran up the steps to the porch and grabbed her. It never even occurred to me she wouldn't know who I was. I left a young boy and I came home an old man. I startled her, but then she knew. We couldn't hold each other long enough. There is something about a mother's arms, the way she holds her child."

Catherine let go of his hand to pull the cocktail napkin from under her drink and dab her eyes.

"You're making me cry and giving me goose bumps."

"Well, there were plenty of tears there on the porch that day, too."

"I'm sure there were."

The flight attendant stopped, and seeing Catherine crying, handed her a couple of napkins. "Is there anything I can get for you two?" she asked.

Zane spoke right up. "No, we really are fine, but thank you."

Catherine squeezed Zane's arm. "I wish I knew what fine was. I don't think I will ever really feel 100 percent fine again."

"Maybe no one does, honey. Maybe our history teaches us how nothing lasts forever and every day is a gift."

"I've heard that before, and maybe you're right. Maybe all we have is today, so we should simply sit in it and enjoy it."

"That's why it was so important for me to bring you to Montana. I don't want to waste another day without you knowing what my life was like. I want you to see and feel what I've experienced, but more importantly, I want my mother and Iron Crow to experience you."

"I'm a little nervous. I hope they aren't expecting too much."

"Catherine, they're going to love you and you are going to love them."

"I don't want to disappoint you."

"How could you? In what way? Be yourself. You know no one on this planet is perfect, which leads me in to the next part of what I have recently discovered. It fits right in with having no expectations."

"Well, that sounds interesting."

"You have no clue. When I was a little kid, I knew Iron Crow was always guarding me. If I went off by myself, especially on my pony, I knew he was tailing me. I thought it was my father who wanted him to keep me safe. When I got older, at times I tried to lose him, but the scoundrel would always outmaneuver or outthink me. He had this sixth sense about him. He was paramount to the overall running of the ranch, too. He kept the ranch hands in line and oversaw the general maintenance and running of the operations. I knew Foster had a lot of respect for and depended on him in a lot ways."

Scared Truths

"So does he still do all that now that he is older?"

"Yes, he's pretty much in charge of everything, although he has a ranch foreman now. Anyway, I hadn't been back very long when I noticed my mother and Iron Crow were a heck of a lot more familiar than I remembered."

"What do you mean?"

"They were shooting glances at each other, and I could feel an undercurrent that was bothering me. It didn't take them long to fill me in on what was going on, and it was a real shocker."

"Will you please tell me? You are killing me building the suspense like this."

"It wasn't like I didn't have a sense there was something unique between those two, even when I was a kid, but I never expected them to tell me what they did."

"Zane, please."

He was grinning at her with that twinkle in his eyes.

"It turns out Iron Crow is my biological father. All those years those two kept it from me. I was shocked."

"So, your mother and Iron Crow . . . Oh, my goodness!"

"Yes. It was like a giant wall of heat hit me. First came the shock of what they said, then came the disbelief, and then came the anger. I had suffered so much watching Foster abuse my mother verbally and physically. He had been so mean to me, and there was always this edge between us. Suddenly, all of it made sense. I was so pissed off I couldn't talk to either of them for a while. Even now, I'm not sure how to feel about the secrecy and the deceit."

"I hate to say this, Zane, but in a way, you got a little dose of your own medicine. I mean maybe you can understand how I felt now. It hurts. It hurts to the core when you think something is and it isn't."

"I do understand. I mean, I never expected them to tell me that, and yet I think deep inside I always knew. There were signs, but I left home when I turned eighteen. I ran with Buck to get away from Foster, and here he wasn't even my father at all. It took me a while to process it, but it still didn't seem right how they kept it from me all those years."

"Well, Zane, in their defense, you were the one who stayed away so long. But then, how long has your so-called father been deceased? Has he been gone all that long? Maybe they had to wait for him to pass."

"I know. I do see their perspective. There were a lot of variables, but it was hard to think it through. I did have a long talk with Iron Crow, and he helped me process some of it. Still, I'm not sure part of it isn't still walled off."

"Boy, do I understand. If I allowed myself to feel all of what I want to feel toward James and Roger . . . . And now I can't get over how they are both in rehab and fighting to get even part of their lives back. It seems ironic and yet . . . . oh, I don't even want to go there."

"I know. I don't want to think too much about all the scenarios either because I really don't want to be mad at my parents. They made a lot of sacrifices."

"Oh, and you think you didn't? You were the one who left home."

"Yes, but they were the ones who allowed me to go. They could have made it difficult for me. My mother never once begged me to come home."

The pilot announced they would be landing shortly. Zane handed their empty glasses to the flight attendant, they put their trays up, and adjusted their seats to the upright positions.

"Well, another leg on this trip is complete, and then I will be introducing you to them. I still have a few things to tell you before we get there."

Zane leaned over and kissed her on the cheek.

"Thank you for being who you are," he said.

Catherine smiled at him as the plane began its descent.

~~~~~

Zane and Catherine had some time during their layover, so they found a quiet corner in a nice airport restaurant and had a bite to eat. Afterwards, they checked to see if their connecting flight was on time and sat across from their boarding gate, waiting.

"I'm glad you told me about your parents' situation. I wouldn't have wanted to meet them and wonder what was going on or have you shoot me looks. It would have made me uncomfortable."

"After I had a little time to myself to think, everything began to fit like a puzzle. The pieces finally made sense. I still don't get why my mother defends Foster, but she says he was her way to a different life. She didn't want to stay on the reservation. Now look at them. She and Iron Crow have the ranch they worked so hard for. It's a shame they are on the downslide now."

"Let's pray they have long lives, Zane. Do you think there were times when they enjoyed themselves despite their situation? I mean, and forgive me for this, but all of my history with James wasn't bad. There were times when we had wonderful moments and trips and memories. I'm sure it may have been the same with them."

"Oh, I agree. I look at it now from their perspective, and I see what they were working toward. I am grateful they have each other openly now."

"What else did you want to tell me?"

"Remember the story about the cave? The one you wrote about. Well, I rode up there alone. I had no idea whether I would go in or not. I simply wanted to be that little boy and experience the area again."

They were calling for first class to board, so Zane rounded up their coats, pulled out their tickets, and steered Catherine by her elbow toward the gate.

"I had a pretty good idea Iron Crow would be tailing me, but I swear to you, I couldn't find him. I tried backtracking and I looked for him when I was higher up on the mesa, but I couldn't see any trace of him or a horse."

"So, did you go in the cave?"

"No. I hobbled my horse and then fell asleep against a warm rock. The next thing I knew, something was dripping on my face. The scoundrel had snuck up above me on the ledge and was dripping water down on me. My horse didn't even give him away."

They handed their tickets to the flight attendant, and walked down the corridor. The flight attendant greeted them at the door of the plane and they found their seats in first class. Zane stuffed their coats and carry-ons in the overhead.

"Then what happened?" Catherine asked with a questioning look as she fastened her seat belt.

"He took me around the backside of the mountain, and showed me a large pile of rocks. Okay now, I may get choked up about this. It was the site where he buried my pony, White Cloud. I don't know if I told you, but when I was a boy, my father sold my pony to the neighbors without even telling me he was going to do it. I had caught the pony and trained him myself. It was heart-wrenching for me."

"How old were you?" Catherine rubbed the top of his hand lovingly.

"I don't remember exactly, but I know I barely reached my mother's waist when she pulled me to her. I remember crying into her skirt and Iron Crow lifting me up and taking me out of the house."

"I'm sorry. What a terrible thing for that man to do!" She squeezed his arm.

"Iron Crow took me right up to the sweet grass area and we caught a horse that time, but it was bittersweet. I hadn't been prepared to give up my pony. It hurt me deeply. Iron Crow told me that after I left, he found out the kids had lost interest in the pony, so he secretly brought him back to the ranch, and turned him out with the herd, high up on the mesa. Foster never knew. Iron Crow kept a check on him and was there with him when he died. He went up there to be with him often, and added rocks each time. I wish you could have seen it."

"I will, Zane. It will be one of the things we do while we're there. We can do that." There were tears sitting on her lower lids about to slide down her cheeks so she pulled a tissue from her pocket.

Zane choked down the lump in his throat and said, "It made me realize how hard this has been for Iron Crow. I was his son, but he couldn't ever acknowledge it, and there he was with me every single day for eighteen years. I suppose he took care of my pony because he couldn't take care of me."

"He must be an extremely strong man."

"He is strong and strong-willed to have put up with the things Foster did and said."

"We do what we have to do. I admire him already and can't wait to meet them both."

"You're like that, Catherine. You kept getting hit with wave after wave, but you came back to take on even more. I'm so sorry you felt I deceived you. It wasn't my intention."

"My mother always said hindsight is a virtue. I never understood what she was talking about really. If only we knew . . . ."

"Yes, but if we had known, would we have taken the same path? I'm not sure."

"One thing certain to me now is you never intentionally set out to hurt me. Neither did James. Your parents certainly didn't intentionally set out to hurt you, either. They were trying to give you the best possible life. Foster didn't intend to be so mean. I'm sure the circumstances made him bitter like I became bitter toward people like Roger and Arianne, and especially James. It is what it is, and we can't go back and change it, can we?" Catherine shrugged her shoulders and straightened herself in the seat.

"No, certainly not, but now I have this opportunity to take you home with me. I'm excited."

"I am too, Zane."

He straightened in his seat as the captain announced they were ready for takeoff. The plane bumped along the runway. Zane braced his head against the headrest as the engines gained power and the plane ascended.

CHAPTER 21

As far as James could tell, Roger hadn't identified him. The poor bastard looked like hell. He probably would have been better off if he had died. In some ways, James wished they had both died. This was no way to try to gain some sort of life again. The therapies were grueling, and he hated being around all these people. He especially disliked having them touch him, help him bathe, and remind him to brush his teeth. Maybe having a worse brain injury would have been a blessing. Then he wouldn't be so damn angry. His body simply wasn't cooperating with what he wanted to do.

Roger was worse off. He didn't appear able to speak clearly, and he was paralyzed on one side. The sons of bitches who had died from his drug concoction were lucky. Ironic they had both ended up in such terrible shape. Maybe the karma thing really did exist. When he was a kid, James had prayed karma would work on some of his foster parents, but it never had. Now he wondered if he wasn't getting a dose of his own damn medicine.

He also wondered about Catherine. He couldn't help himself. She had been the one good thing in his life, but he had completely screwed it up. He hadn't even thought of the consequences she would face by his decisions. Hindsight was tearing him apart. The *if onlys* constantly ate at him. He had come to the conclusion it stemmed from his being all alone in the world at such an early age. The orphanage and then being passed from home to home had made him shut down. He had learned to stuff his feelings far deeper than he had realized. Catherine had been the only glimmer of light in a very dark series of events.

As a teen, he had thought of suicide, but he was afraid he would screw it up. Now look what he'd done. The thing he feared had happened. Too bad his drug concoction hadn't come earlier in his life. Then none of this would have occurred. Maybe his sorry ass would have been six feet under and he wouldn't have messed up Catherine's precious life. The thought of her tormented him. He tried not to think of her in bed with the piece of crap cowboy. She deserved someone better than him.

His ongoing mental dialogue was interrupted when they rolled Roger into the dining room, and placed him directly across the table from him. It seemed to be James' rotten luck that he'd have to watch them feed him. The worst part was he couldn't protest or make a scene or he would draw attention or suspicion to himself. He couldn't escape the constant reminder of what Roger and he had done, not only to Catherine, but to themselves. It sucked.

~~~~~

Roger had finally figured out why the guy sitting across from him looked so familiar. He looked a lot like his old college roommate, but then he didn't. It was frustrating trying to pull it together. He wanted to ask him what college he'd attended, but he was still having a lot of trouble getting words to come out so that anyone could understand them.

His body was finally beginning to respond to the therapies. His arms didn't feel like they weighed a hundred pounds, and he was gaining control of their movement. His current goal was to feed himself and to stop drooling. He was sick to death of people having to bathe him, wipe his ass, and dress him—the whole nine yards. It was embarrassing. These people had no idea with whom they were dealing. Christ, he didn't even know who he had been. He remembered bits and pieces. Memories were coming back slowly. Snapshots of images entered like photographs. He remembered tall buildings. A closet full of suits, of all things. And he remembered a beautiful, dark-haired woman.

They were working hard to teach him to write. The speech therapist he liked the most told him maybe the words would come easier if he could put them together in a sentence on paper. He liked the way she smelled. He looked across the table at the familiar man, then got distracted by someone with his tray of food.

"Well, honey, how are you doing today? Let's get you some supper. Okay?"

Soon he wouldn't have to do this. Soon he would hold a fork and knife and feed himself. They would see.

~~~~

Bill Brannan called Dr. Finley and informed him the two men under his care had been former college roommates. He didn't tell him much about their connection with NSA, but he told him to be aware they might or might not still be friends. NSA wanted to know if they had shown any indication that they knew each other, and whether they had opportunities to converse.

Dr. Finley had stayed within the parameters of patient confidentiality, but told Brannan that Roger was currently unable to communicate well with anyone, and as far as he knew, the two patients had no direct contact with each other. He assured him he would instruct the staff to monitor the two closely and report any unusual behaviors or actions.

"Excellent," Bill Brannan said. "Keep me posted."

"Yes, I certainly will."

~~~~

Dr. Finley stood with his back propped against the wall and wrote Bill's information in a little black book he carried in his pocket. He hadn't taken to using his phone the way some of the interns did.

Later, Dr. Finley asked the staff to position the two men at meals across from each other as a way to stimulate their interests, since they seemed to come from similar backgrounds. He didn't feel there was any need for the staff to be aware of their situation. Cameras were streaming all day long throughout the facility, so if there was anything unusual reported, Dr. Finley could review the videos. He could only hope these men would have favorable outcomes in their recoveries, but they were both struggling at this point. He walked down the hall and into security.

"Hello, Walter. Can you show me the dining room monitor?" he asked.

"This one right here, Doc. How you doing today?"

"Perfect. Want to monitor a couple of my patients. Can you zoom in on this table right here?"

"You got it, Doc."

As Dr. Finley had expected, James and Roger weren't interacting at all. He continued to watch them for a few minutes, until he saw the aide arrive with the tray to feed Roger.

"Thanks, Walter. If I need to monitor these two patients, would it be a big deal?"

"Not at all. Meals are pretty much on schedule, so you tell me what days you want and I can pull them up and put them on a CD or flash drive for you. Then, you can review them at your leisure."

"Splendid. I'll let you know if I need you to do that. Take it easy."

"You too, Doc. Are you doing okay?"

"You bet."

CHAPTER 22

Zane and Catherine made their way through the airport and down the escalator to baggage claim. They hadn't packed much. Zane had told her whatever they didn't have or need, they would buy. It didn't take long for their bags to appear. They headed toward the rental car counter.

"Do you care who we rent the car from?" he asked.

"Not at all."

He steered her toward Hertz and pulled a credit card out of his wallet.

"Do you want me . . . ?" she started to ask, but he wasn't about to let her pay for anything. Not on this trip.

"My town, my treat," he interrupted her.

"But—"

"No argument. My rules."

"How do you do it?"

"What?"

"That grin. You used it the first time I met you. Even in the dull morning light along the side of the road, I could see it. You charmed me with that grin of yours."

"I assure you I didn't know or I would have taken advantage of it."

The man behind the counter ignored their banter.

"Sir, what size vehicle do you want? Economy, compact, mid-size, or SUV?"

"My lady would like an SUV?"

Catherine smiled at him, tucking her arm in his.

"Hey," Zane told her, "I figured if you and my mother want to go anywhere, you'll be comfortable driving a vehicle you're familiar with. Besides, we don't need to be bumping around in a truck. I can borrow one from the ranch if I need it."

"Thank you. I think it would be lovely if your mother and I spent some alone time together."

"Well, believe me, if you decide to go somewhere off the ranch, it will take you most of the day, so you will have plenty of alone time while you're driving. The ranch isn't close to anything."

The man behind the counter handed Zane his credit card, offered a pen, and motioned for him to sign the papers. He creased the copies, placed them in a folder, and gave them their set of keys.

"Your vehicle is in parking spot 17, straight out the west doors, Mr. Wheeler."

Zane nodded at the man. They made their way around the corner and out the sliding doors with their bags. A gust of wind caught them both by surprise.

"I forgot about the velocity of the wind out here. It nearly pushed me back through the doors," Catherine said.

"That's because we're facing west into it. Can you smell it?"

"What?"

"The sweet grass."

"Not really."

"Wait." He took a deep breath.

~~~~~

Catherine was surprised when Zane pulled off the main road and into a restaurant parking lot.

"Thought maybe we would grab a bite to eat and then call my momma and tell her when we'll arrive."

"Sounds great to me. We have no set schedule unless you're anxious to get to your folks."

"All in good time, my dear. I'm simply ecstatic we are together in Montana. This restaurant has been here for forty forevers. Always get a fabulous meal here."

The restaurant was similar to the Country Kettles her mother had taken them to when they went off on their vacations. However, while they waited to be seated, Catherine couldn't quite get over the stuffed goat and mountain lion in a definite life or death pose in the middle of the dining room.

"That's interesting," she said defensively.

"It's for the tourists," Zane explained. "They love the wilderness theme. I swear I think some of them want to be attacked by a grizzly bear."

"They do not," she protested.

"Oh yes they do. Then they can go home—"

"Stop teasing me."

The hostess interrupted them, leading them to a table in the opposite direction of the display.

"I guess she read my mind," Catherine winked at him.

Zane chuckled.

"Are you using your extra-sensory perception stuff on her? You were probably mouthing it and she read your lips. 'Take me away from this thing.' Right?"

"Stop. I don't want to laugh. I was trying to wait until I ordered before I slipped away to the lady's room."

"Go. Tell me what you want and go. You don't need to sit here. I know what you're going to order. Chicken. You always order chicken."

~~~~~

"Whew, now I feel better," Catherine said as she slid into the booth next to him. She hated to admit it, but she had been really tired from the long day of sitting in airports and on planes. This had been a good idea to relax and recharge.

"Thank you, Zane. I really needed this kind of a break. You were right. We will feel refreshed when I meet your parents."

Scared Truths

They finished their meal and headed out to the parking lot.

"Let's call my mother before we get in the car. I may have to wander around to get a signal."

It wouldn't be long before Catherine would be meeting Zane's parents. She had never expected things to turn out like this. She leaned against the side of the car and gazed west. It was going to be a beautiful evening to drive toward his past and their future. Only time would tell what the outcome would be, but if she had learned one thing through all of this, it was to have no expectations.

~~~~~

Zane and Catherine had been driving in silence, heading north of Great Falls, when she simply couldn't contain her emotions another minute. As tears began to slide silently down her face, she grabbed her purse on the seat next to her and fumbled around in it.

"Do you need something?" Zane asked.

She tried not to let him know she was crying, but she was certain he would hear it in her voice if she said anything. She cleared her throat.

"I'm fine. Think the airport made my head a little stuffy," she lied as she located a tissue and blew her nose, hoping he wouldn't notice as she wiped her tears.

"Are you crying?"

"Maybe a little."

"Are you okay?"

"I don't get it. There are such wide-open spaces here. It's beautiful and mostly unpopulated."

"You mean you don't get why more people don't live here? The winters are pretty rough. You know, temperatures way below zero. It isn't easy or for everyone."

She wanted to say yes, it was about that, but her heart was tearing apart. They had promised to be honest with each other.

"No. I don't get why they couldn't get along. There is so much land and so much space, so why didn't they let the Native

Americans continue to live here. Why the genocide? What was so wrong with where and how they lived? I don't understand it. They murdered them for no reason."

Catherine sniffled and blew her nose again. "It's heartbreaking. What did they do? They were living quietly and taking care of their families and each other. They respected nature and the natural flow of everything. Were the people who came so greedy they had to completely annihilate them?"

"Have you ever heard of a virgin soil epidemic?"

"A what?"

"Well, it wasn't only the murdering and removal; it was also being exposed to diseases they had never faced before. They were immunologically almost defenseless. The Europeans brought with them lethal things like smallpox, measles, flu, and whooping cough, to name a few. Then the bastards even took blankets from the quarantined smallpox military infirmary and handed them out to the Indians. Can you imagine what kind of people could even come up with that or would want to do it? Some say this affected up to ninety-five percent of the Native American population."

"I've done some research on this, but it still tears me apart to hear the numbers."

"I know. When the adults all became sick at once or died, there was so much hunger and starvation that in some cases an entire tribe was wiped out."

"Do you really think the spreading of disease was intentional? Or was it simply part of what happened when the Europeans invaded the continent?"

"Wow, that's a good term. I never heard anyone refer to it as an invasion, but it sums it up. They invaded the continent. And, in answer to your question, I think it was definitely a combination of things, but one thing is certain—none of it was favorable for the Native American population."

"Either way, it makes me sad. Why couldn't they have all gotten along?"

"The eternal question. We never learn, do we?"

"I don't think so," Catherine said, sniffling.

There was silence for a long time as she stared out the window at what Zane had called coulees. She imagined what it had been like to live on such a large continent and have no safe place.

"Why do they call them coulees?" she asked.

"It's a land form, like a dry gully or ravine. Why do you ask?"

"I was thinking about the women and children running from the soldiers down in the coulees. I read something about that. It's making me feel extremely sad."

~~~~

"Let's stop here and let me stretch my legs," Zane said, pulling into a rest area.

Catherine giggled.

"What are you laughing at?"

"Why don't men say they have to go to the bathroom? It's funny. Or you say you have to take a leak. But then we say we have to use the powder room."

"I'm sure you do have to use the powder room. You've been quiet and deep in thought or are you simply tired?"

"A little of both. I never realized seeing the plains would make me feel things so deeply. It has hit my heart really hard."

"Well then, you can imagine how my mother feels. Her ancestors have been on this planet for over five thousand years. She has deep, deep roots."

"I can't even comprehend how she feels."

"You can ask her. She will be more than willing to share with you about her heritage and how they've learned to deal with the changes they had to make."

"I don't want to upset her by asking."

"You won't upset her. It's a part of her history. Her people survived, and they are proud to still be here. That's another reason why she and Iron Crow wanted to live differently than on the reservation. They are grateful for what the land gives them. You will see. Then you'll know."

Zane got out and strode across the parking lot and into the building. Catherine followed him, heading in the opposite direction to the ladies' room. She couldn't believe how stiff she felt from sitting all day. She couldn't wait to get to the ranch and move around.

"Where are we?" Catherine asked when they both arrived back at the car.

"Choteau, Teton County, Montana. They say it's the gateway to the Rocky Mountains. Small town."

"It seems quaint."

"Mostly agricultural, but don't know about quaint. Not a big population. Maybe a thousand. We are less than an hour away from the ranch."

"Are you getting excited to see them again?"

"Yes. Are you excited to meet them?"

"Of course, I am. And a little nervous."

"No need to be. They will treat you like a princess."

"And you a prince?" She shot him a sideways glance and smiled.

"Always. You will be very comfortable with them once you get over the initial jitters. Don't worry. It will be fine."

They were back on the road again in silence. He glanced at her without moving his head and realized she was staring dead ahead.

"Where are you?"

"Oh, I was wondering why there were such conflicts? Weren't there enough resources for all of them to survive? Then I was seeing the images of the women and children running along these coulees trying to get away from the soldiers. I can feel it. It's quite disturbing."

"I didn't think the history of this place would affect you like this."

"I don't understand it myself. I feel this overwhelming sadness, and I feel almost like it's déjà vu. Like I experienced it. It's making me feel uncomfortable. It seems like I can see things, feel things that happened here. I'm having to hold back my tears again."

"Maybe you are so sensitive that you're picking up the energy of the area. And you're right. There were a lot of conflicts all over this region. In fact, the Blackfeet were a very peaceful people, but to protect themselves, they made it appear that they were much meaner and ruthless than they were. Few settlers traveled through Blackfeet land due to their reputation."

"I didn't know. I thought they were one of the most violent tribes."

"The tribal people wanted the newcomers to be afraid of them because they were determined not to give up their land. The reservation is about one and a half million acres. They are one of the only tribes who kept their land."

"I don't understand—with all this vastness, why?"

"The United States government hired hunters to kill off the buffalo. Without their primary food source, the tribal peoples could be controlled and contained. It's how they were forced onto reservations. Basically, they starved them. Add the destruction from the diseases the Europeans brought to this country, and they didn't have a chance. They have never recovered. You can see the evidence of it on most reservations."

"It's making me feel sick to my stomach."

"Like I said, I had no idea the energy would affect you like this."

"I know. I feel like I know so little about this part of history, yet my emotions and my body are telling me it is deeply imbedded in my soul."

"Take a breath. Here, I'll turn the radio on and maybe we can change the atmosphere in here to give you a break."

He found a clear station playing country music.

"Do you like to hear flute music?" he asked.

"Funny you should ask. I wanted to play the flute, but at the time, my mother couldn't afford to buy me one, and the school only had one, and some girl claimed it first."

"That's sad. The reason I was asking is Iron Crow had a friend who played this wooden flute, and the melodies he played were haunting. I will have to ask him about it. Iron Crow also plays."

They had driven for almost an hour when Zane slowed the truck and turned left through a wooden fence and over a cattle grate. It made a rattling sound and startled Catherine.

"What was that?"

"A cattleguard. The cows are afraid of it because it's open underneath, so they won't step across it."

"Really? That's the only thing keeping them in?"

"Yep; it's worked for all these years."

"I find it perplexing. Why are they afraid? I think there's one at my gate at the farm, but I never knew what it was."

"Silly critters. They balk at it because they don't want to get their legs stuck between the pipes. And yes, you do have one."

"What are you smiling at?"

"You. You know so much and yet you know so little."

"Stop. I simply haven't been exposed to the ranch world the way you have."

"Well, there you go. And you, my love, are about to enter into an amazing new adventure."

Zane reached over and squeezed Catherine's hand.

"I'm excited to meet your mother."

"And I'm certain she's excited to meet you."

He glanced in the rearview mirror at the truck kicking up the usual dust from the gravel road. This was about to be one of the happiest days of his life. He was bringing the two women he loved more than anything else in the world together at a place he had longed to be for a very long time.

CHAPTER 23

It had taken one phone call and Buck Matthews was about to sign a contract for the sale of his feed store. His customer had mentioned if he ever wanted to sell the store, he would be interested. At the time, Buck had no clue his life would be taking yet another turn.

Wallace Purdy would make a fine new owner. He had moved to Highberry recently from upstate New York. After working for someone else for ten years and fighting the horrible winters, the middle-aged man was excited to be his own boss. Buck couldn't be happier. He'd even given Wallace permission to keep the old name—All Around Feed. What the hell did he care? He'd be one happy camper not to be stuck in the store all day six days a week. He could get on to another life.

Buck told Wallace, "I don't give a flying pig what you call it." He didn't even care if he lost money on the sale. He simply wanted to get on with the move before the weather changed. Wallace hadn't even quibbled with him. Paid him cash from his mother's estate. Damnedest thing.

Autumn would be the perfect time to resettle his family to the Montana ranch so they would get acclimated before the snow began. Now all they needed was a contract on the house. Once Zane and Catherine returned from their trip, Buck's parents would be heading back to Montana. He knew if his dad didn't have any animals to care for, he'd be chomping at the bit for something to do.

Buck was thanking his lucky stars he didn't have any livestock to sell. They didn't even have a dog. It had all worked out much better than he could have planned. Now, if the house would sell right away, they'd be in heaven. The only thing he wished he'd done was send Deb and the kids to see her parents before she was way the hell in the North Country.

Deb had already started sorting through things and boxing up some items she wanted to take. They hadn't lived together that long, which was a bonus, because they hadn't accumulated much. Buck hadn't been there long enough to have the usual man cave stuff, plus he and Zane had been vagabonds in their careers, keeping the house fairly simple.

~~~~~

Deb was upstairs working in the hall closet when Buck arrived home from work. She had completely lost track of time. Not that it mattered. Buck's mother had dinner simmering on the stove. She could smell it. Roan had been playing some game with the twins, keeping them occupied, so she had decided to sort through the linens. There were two sets of sheets for each bed and a bunch of bath towels, hand towels, and washcloths. The rest of it was pretty much rags and cleaning supplies. When she shut the door and turned around, he grabbed her.

"You about scared me half to death," she said as he wrapped his arms around her. He tried to kiss her, but she ducked.

"Sorry. I thought you heard me come up the steps."

"No, I had my head in there." She pointed to the closet. "It's not going to be too bad moving. We don't have much to pack."

"I travel light."

"Yes, I guess we both do. I've never settled long in one place either."

She hesitated for a moment. Maybe she should tell him— tell him her life had been very similar to his. How she'd moved around a lot. Working for the government had required it. That she was one of them. But she leaned back and simply looked long and hard into his eyes.

"Want to mess around?" he asked.

"Oh, my goodness, with your parents downstairs, right now?"

"Why not? They're busy. We could—"

She stopped him.

"You know how . . . ."

She hesitated. Even though she had felt so comfortable with him, it was difficult for her to relax with other people in the house.

"Do you think they don't do it?" he asked.

"Oh, Buck." She tried to shush him.

"At least they did do it. I'm living proof." He grinned at her.

"Stop. It's not that. What if one of the kids wants us? I'm more comfortable when they're asleep."

"We could do it in the shower."

"Let's wait. Your folks need to get back to Catherine's, and I don't want anyone to come looking for us. And besides, there's something I want to talk to you about."

She'd wanted to have this conversation for a long time. She took his hand and walked into their bedroom.

"You're taking me to the wrong place if you want to talk. I'm warning you."

"Stop. This will only take a couple of minutes. I promise. We can do something tonight after the kids are asleep."

He sighed and sat down on the bed.

"At least sit on my lap."

He pulled her down and kissed her.

"This is hard for me," Deb said, "because I don't like keeping things from you, so I hope you understand."

"Sounds serious." Buck looked at her with his forehead wrinkled.

"Maybe a little. You know we met when I was a realtor and I kept pestering you by bringing people into the feed store. Right?"

"Yes, of course I do."

"Well, there's more to the story."

"I'm all ears," he said and tried to nibble on her ear lobe.

"Can you stop for a minute? This is hard for me to tell you."

"I'm excited about the move, selling the feed store, and the kids and us are gonna—"

Deb put her fingers on his lips.

"Okay, honey, focus for a minute."

Buck raised his eyebrows and smiled.

"I had another life before I moved to Highberry."

"We all did."

"You aren't making this easy. Yes, we all had different lives, but mine wasn't in real estate. I worked with Bill Brannan and some of the guys you and Zane worked with."

"What?" Buck took her shoulders and pushed her away from him, staring into her face.

"I wanted to tell you before, but there wasn't the right moment. And now since we're moving, and we've been together this long, well . . . I want to come clean and for us to start our new lives without anything hidden."

"And . . . ."

"They kept me pretty much out of the country. I speak several languages, so they used me for a lot of different missions. I could get in and out of situations easier than the guys since I could wear burkas and scarves and conceal myself. There were a lot of pluses to being female and a lot of women who helped me."

"Okay, is there anything else you need to tell me?"

"What? No, I don't think so. You don't seem upset or surprised."

"Well, do you want me to tell the truth now?"

"Of course, I do. I want us to be upfront from now on."

"Well, from now on, our life is going to be pretty simplistic. We are going to be raising our kids out in the middle of nowhere, and all we're going to do is watch them grow up and tend to the ranch. There won't be anything to hide. Besides, the truth is, I knew. I've known for a while. Bill Brannan paid me a visit at the feed store when he found out you and I were an item to warn me about you."

Deb raised her voice as she said, "He did what? He warned you about me? What did he say?"

"Oh, he told me what kind of woman you were."

"What does that mean? What did he say?" She was leaning back on his lap, letting her bristles come up and becoming defensive.

"I'm teasing you," Buck said, smiling. "He wanted me to know who you really were and what I was getting myself into. By then, I didn't really care what he said because I had fallen in love with you. Our kids were a bonus. It didn't matter what you had been. I loved who we were together. It all seemed surreal for a while—a man of my age with my terrible track record with women landing a beautiful woman like you and us expecting twins. It blew me away. Once I knew for sure about you, then what you'd done made sense."

"Like what?"

"Well, admit it. When we first met you weren't all that attractive. You wore a lot of makeup and those flowing, baggy clothes. You reminded me of some kind of gypsy."

"I didn't want to be attractive. I had a job to do."

"And you did it well. But then we had that one night, and the next thing I knew, your appearance changed. You were looking different. But then you know the rest of this story."

"So do you have regrets?"

"Regrets? Hell, no. I'm happy." He rubbed his prickly whiskers on her neck.

She giggled, and he kissed her.

"Are you upset with me for not telling you myself?"

"What difference did it make? I had found your hidden cellphone and your badge one day in the closet. Then Bill turned up and filled in the remainder of the blanks. I could have run a search on you any time. It didn't matter. Wouldn't have mattered. People change. Times change. Everything morphs into something else."

"I'm grateful you felt that way. I wanted to tell you. I was attracted to you from the beginning. And now, well, you and the kids complete me."

"I think I heard that in a movie."

As she wrapped her arms around his neck, he said, "And there's something I want to tell you. I think you need to take our two kids and go see your parents before we are halfway across the country from them. You should take my mother with you to help with the kids on the plane so you don't have to travel alone. We can well afford a hotel suite or whatever you need at the other end to accommodate the four of you. Get a rental car. Do whatever you need, but make plans now to go see them. I'm hoping the house will sell as fast as the feed store and we can be packed up and gone before the weather changes too drastically out west."

"I love you so much, Buck Matthews. You are the most generous man and the greatest daddy in the world."

"Well, I have my parents to thank for that."

"I hate to make your mom travel with us, but she's so good with the kids. Do you think she will go?"

"I think she would love it. And my dad can help me with things around here while all of you are gone."

"Well, then, we can ask her at dinner before they go back to Catherine's house, and I'll call my folks in the morning after I figure out a plan."

She grabbed his face in her hands and kissed him.

"And right now, we have to get back downstairs."

"Okay, okay we'll go," he said as he reluctantly let her go.

CHAPTER 24

Catherine gasped as they turned a corner and came out of a deep coulee. A long lane passed under an entrance constructed of the largest, most beautiful poles she had ever seen. Across the top pole was a series of metal horses and cattle. On either side were giant wheels placed about halfway down the poles, and across the top in large black letters was the name Wheeler.

"Wow, that's really some entrance."

"Foster had to have the best always."

"It looks like it was built yesterday."

"He took pride in the maintenance of the ranch. I'm pretty sure he had the thing cleaned and repaired twice a year—spring and fall. Wait until you see the house."

"So, it's still called Wheeler?" she asked, hesitantly.

"I'm sure they left it out of respect. Their lives were so entwined. I'm pretty sure they won't take it down. You'll find them to be fairly passive in some ways. That would seem too radical to them, I suppose."

"You would think they'd want to get rid of everything about him."

"He will always be a part of this ranch. He made it all possible. They would never take that away from him. What would be the point?"

"That's what's hard for me, Zane, with my situation. I want to erase what I knew about *him*. I don't even want to mention his name."

"But your situation was different than theirs. They were all working toward the same goal: the ranch."

"And you. This whole thing happened because of you, too. That's the difference. In my situation, he didn't really think things through, and that changed our lives drastically. He excluded me."

"Well, their lives were changed a lot when I fled."

She took a deep breath.

"Life certainly dishes out things we aren't expecting, and maybe we never do figure them out."

"Maybe so, but here we are now. I'm excited for you to get to know them."

Zane's eyes were sparkling, and he had a different energy about him. Catherine could feel it.

"I'm glad to see you this excited, Zane."

"It's different coming home like this. It finally all makes sense, and here you are with me. I can't explain it. I want to slow it down and enjoy every moment. I can't erase the past because it was, but I am looking forward to our spending this time together with them."

Catherine gasped again as they came closer to the house. "Oh, my God, Zane. It's astounding."

"I know, and I got to live here."

A veranda ran the entire way around the house with a beautiful wooden handrail. The huge poles were very similar to the ones at the entrance gate. The second floor had wonderful dormer windows. The entire house was perched on rock pillars, and it looked like there was a basement underneath. Catherine could see small windows between the pillars and the rock. A large stone chimney stood on each end of the house.

"Two chimneys?" she asked, her head darting back and forth from Zane to the house.

"Um, it does get pretty damn cold out here."

"Wow, that's a big house."

"I don't think it's much bigger than your house. It looks bigger since it's sitting out in the middle of nowhere."

"It sure looks big to me."

"Maybe it's the big sky." He winked at her. "You know."

"Okay, I get it. Big sky Montana. It's unbelievably beautiful."

Catherine was still staring at the house when Zane stepped hard on the brake, brought the SUV to a dusty stop, and put it in park.

"We're here!"

Zane hadn't made it around to Catherine's side of the Lincoln when the front door opened and two people came out onto the front porch. He reached in and pulled her into his arms, then carried her up the front steps, depositing her in front of his mother. Catherine had to hang on to him to get her balance for a second.

"Catherine, may I present my mother, Maggie White Calf, and this guy here would be my father, Parker Iron Crow."

Catherine stuck out her hand, and his mother took it, gently pulling Catherine into her arms.

"We are so pleased to have you here at our home, Catherine. Welcome!"

Catherine had never been hugged so softly and fully before. It felt overwhelming. Iron Crow took her by her shoulders and turned her toward him, looking straight into her eyes.

"Catherine, we are so happy to have you here with us."

Iron Crow and Maggie both turned and motioned toward the two large wooden open doors. Zane had to nudge her to get her feet to move. She felt like she was walking into a movie set. It barely felt real. The open great room seemed gigantic. The earth tones of the logs and the wooden floor were warm and inviting. There were accents of color—turquoise pillows, a coral throw, and two deep emerald green vases on the fireplace. The huge coffee table in the middle of the two angled couches was made from a large slice of a tree trunk and polished to perfection.

His mother said, "Zane, let's all go out to the kitchen. I know that's your favorite place to be. You must be thirsty and hungry. I'll fix you something. We'll get your bags after."

The kitchen smelled delicious. A mix of what Catherine thought must be chicken cooking and spices. The huge table was long and equally as beautiful as the coffee table, but worn and well used. Long benches were on either side and beautiful wooden carved chairs at either end.

"The ranch hands eat their meals in here. We treat them as family," Iron Crow said and motioned for them to sit.

Zane pulled out the chair at the end of the table for Catherine.

"Oh, no, I couldn't," she said softly. "I'll be happy sitting on the bench next to you, Zane."

As they all sat, catching up, Catherine was taken aback momentarily by the soft sound of their voices. It lulled her into a calmer place—a place she hadn't been in a long time. In fact, she felt as though she were experiencing something that wasn't quite now—like she'd seen or already been here before. It was hard to comprehend. It was as if she knew these voices, this dialect, this different pattern of speaking. She felt like she had experienced some place similar to this, and yet she knew she hadn't. It was soothing and perplexing at the same time.

They took their time, enjoying a snack, and talked for almost two hours until Catherine was feeling somewhat drained. Zane's mother must have sensed it.

"Okay, let's bring your bags upstairs and you two can take a nap or a bath or rest or whatever you want to do. When you come down, we can spend some time on the porch or whatever you feel up to. I'm happy to have you both here."

Zane and Iron Crow brought the bags in and carried them up the beautiful worn wooden stairs. It was a wider staircase than Catherine had ever seen, and the landing upstairs looked down into the great room. Two chairs, a love seat, and a table created a cozy reading area.

Zane and Catherine's room was spacious and had a private bathroom. His mother had placed a lovely vase of wildflowers on the dresser. Zane told her later they would probably be the last of the season, since the temperatures were dropping at night. Soon the aspen leaves would quake and be gone, and the winter would set in. She didn't even bother to undress, but took off her boots and lay across the bed. Zane snuggled up against her, and they were soon sound asleep.

CHAPTER 25

Catherine sat up in the bed, startled at not knowing where she was for a moment. Zane stirred and then stretched and yawned.

"Oh, my goodness. I haven't slept like that in I don't know how long. I was out completely," Zane said.

"Me, too. I think we both passed out. I wonder what time it is."

"My phone is on the dresser."

Catherine rolled off the bed and picked up his cellphone.

"We've been asleep for almost two hours. We should go downstairs."

She walked into the bathroom, washed her face, and looked in the mirror.

"Did you see the creases in my face?" she asked Zane.

"Not really. I barely have my eyes open." He stretched, stood up, and looked out the upstairs window at the backyard and the mountains off in the distance. "It's a shame I stayed away so long."

"I know, Zane. I don't know why you did."

"It was him. I didn't want any part of him."

"You mean your—what do you want me to call him? I mean he's not your father anymore, is he?"

"I don't know what to call him either. It's strange. I have to stop my brain and think about it too. Foster. His first name was Foster. That even seems strange. When we were on the porch, when we got here, I had to think how to introduce you. It's the first time I've said it out loud, you know, calling Iron Crow my father."

"Well, you honestly can't go back and change anything. Thank God you are here now. That's what matters. And now you know the truth. It has to be such a relief to know and to say it."

"Yes, it makes it all simpler, but it was such a long time coming. I wish she had more years to enjoy it. Seems like my mother got cheated."

"They made their choices the same way you did. No one has a crystal ball. If only we could see the future. But then we wouldn't be who we are; the difficulties help define us. Those hard knocks supposedly made us stronger. Look at the strength of your mother and then how hard this had to be for Iron Crow."

"Let's go down and spend some time with them. I know they are anxious to get to know you."

"I have butterflies in my stomach. I can't believe we are really here."

Zane took her hand and they walked down the beautiful staircase and into the great room.

"I love this room, this house. It's incredible," Catherine said.

"It's a beautiful house. I have to hand it to him. Foster hosted some wonderful parties here. We had a lot of good neighbors, especially the Matthews. I have fond memories of this room and at our kitchen table."

They walked into the kitchen, where his mother was standing at the sink paring potatoes. "Well, there you two are. Did you have a nice nap?"

"Oh, my goodness, yes. I haven't slept so deeply in a long time."

"Mountain air. There's nothing like it. It soothes the soul." Zane's mother smiled at both of them. "Parker said he could take you for a little ride around the ranch in the truck if you would like. He's sitting out there on the back porch. You'll be back in time to have dinner with us and the men. We eat late this time of year. It's your favorite, Zane; a nice fat chicken."

Catherine watched as Zane hugged his mother and kissed her forehead. She could see her in his cheekbones, the twinkle in his eyes, and how he held himself. They moved in a methodical, slow way—soft and flowing.

"Do you want to go for a ride?" he asked Catherine.

"Of course. I'm ready to see whatever you want to show me."

"Well, then we're off."

He kissed his mother on the cheek this time and held the screen door for Catherine. The wind caught her by surprise when she stepped out. It was blowing straight into her face, and the power and the sweetness of the air took her breath away. They found Iron Crow still sitting on the porch. He stood up, pointing toward a truck parked across the yard.

"Want to take a spin in my pony?" He chuckled.

"Of course, we're ready," Zane replied.

"Then here we go. Put her in the front with me so she can see better, and I promise not to throw her through the windshield."

Catherine looked at him with a startled look.

"He's kidding. You'll get used to his left-handed comments. He's reminding me about the time he was teaching me to drive and we didn't use seat belts back then. He was sitting next to me, and I hit the brakes too hard, sending him into the dash. He says I tried to throw him through the windshield. I think I was about eight years old and barely reached the pedals."

Iron Crow shot her a look and winked. They headed straight out of the yard in between two long fence lines. Zane got out to open a gate so Iron Crow could drive through, and from there, they began to climb. They saw a few horses and then came upon a pond where there was a large group of them. Some were in the water and others were either grazing nearby or standing on the bank.

"This is absolutely astounding. They are beautiful. What a special place," she said.

"They call the herd a remuda," Zane told her. "It's a term Foster liked to use. A remuda is where the cowboys choose their mounts. Some days, when we were moving or working the cattle, we would ride for a while and then change horses so we didn't completely sour them to the work. You want your horse to be alert and able to work the cows without injuring itself or you."

"That's interesting. I never thought about that."

"Nowadays, they round them up with all-terrain vehicles and then load them into semi-trucks to haul them, but years ago, we drove them to market or to the train station. It was a really wonderful time for all of us. We camped out along the way, and a cook wagon went along with us."

Iron Crow said, "There were nights around the campfire when tall tales were told. Wannabe musicians had their chance to howl at the moon, and Zane, well, he got to play his harmonica."

"What? You don't mean it. You play a harmonica?"

"Not lately. I haven't played since I left the ranch."

She didn't know what to say. There seemed to be a lot of things he had left behind when he fled this life.

"Didn't you play something?" she asked Iron Crow. "Zane said you play the flute."

Zane answered for him. "He was the storyteller. He played with our minds."

Iron Crow chuckled and looked at her out of the corner of his eye.

"Now I know where you got it from," she told Zane.

"What?" Zane asked.

"The way you look at me without turning your head. The first couple of times you did it, you freaked me out."

"I didn't think you noticed."

"It still kind of freaks me out. I never saw anyone do that before."

"I thought it was normal. Doesn't everyone do it?"

Parker turned, looked at him in the backseat behind Catherine, and said, "Only us, not them."

"Oh, you mean Native Americans do it, but not us white people?" she asked.

They were both grinning at her.

"He's teasing you. I think it is a learned trait. I don't think anyone is born doing it. He taught me how. It used to drive Foster crazy; and, Iron Crow, she's not telling the truth. She's partly one of us."

As they hit a bump, Catherine bounced up and forward and her seat belt tightened. "And who do you suppose taught him how to hit the rough spots?" she said, grabbing on to the seat belt. She was laughing.

"She catches on fast, huh, Zane? And yes, Catherine, I did play the flute."

~~~~~

Maggie White Calf used her sage and sweet grass bundle and smudged the house during the time she was alone. It was her ritual to purify the rooms, banish negativity, and bring in the positive. She didn't want any bad energy around any of the people who would come to her table or sleep in her house, especially Zane and Catherine. She had always loved the scent of it, ever since she was a baby. Her mother had used it often, but apparently not enough. Their life on the reservation had been difficult.

From the time she could remember, a lot of people had always lived in their house—her mother, her siblings, her mother's sister, people she wasn't sure were related, and strange men who came and then were gone. Their house was a place of comings and goings. Something cooking on the stove, someone sleeping on a couch, or even in her bed, at times. And there were plenty of children to play with. It hadn't all been bad, but it hadn't been calm or quiet.

The house had been one of the things Maggie loved the most about the ranch. Once all the men were fed and out, she had the place pretty much to herself all day. She could come, go, and do as she pleased. Naturally, there were always things to do, but Foster Wheeler had left her to her own devices. One thing he hadn't done was boss her about the household chores, and he had been generous with providing her all the things she needed in the kitchen to feed his men. She couldn't fault him on that.

There had also been Maria. It had been a godsend to have her to talk to, woman to woman. Maria helped her tend to the chickens and the garden. She helped with the heavy stuff like toting all the canned vegetables down to the cellar. Whatever she needed, Maria was eager to help. She and her husband had fled Mexico and found a sanctuary on the ranch, too. The two women had the commonality of that.

While Maggie was upstairs, she made the beds, fluffed up the pillows, and refreshed the flowers she'd picked for Catherine. She wasn't surprised by what a nice couple they made. They suited each other. She hoped they could both find peace. They seemed distracted, on edge, not relaxed at all. She was hoping the ranch would have a healing effect on the two of them. The sage and sweet grass would help, but the ranch had to share its secrets too. It was wonderful to have Zane home again. Maggie hurried back downstairs to check on her pies in the oven. In a short while, she would be serving yet another meal.

CHAPTER 26

Dr. Finley was at home taking a quick nap before heading back to the rehab center to do afternoon rounds and paperwork. He jumped and grabbed for the phone. The clock on the nightstand read 2 p.m. His heart was racing in his chest. The voice on the line was screaming at someone.

"Hello. Hello. It's Dr. Finley. Who is this?"

"Oh, sorry, so sorry, Dr. Finley. It's Walter in security, sir. We have had an accident. There was an explosion. They asked me to call you."

"An explosion. Walter, what happened? Where?"

"Here! Right here, sir. I mean the rehab room in the basement. It blew. There was no warning. It's a madhouse. Police and fire units are already here. They are evacuating the entire building. You can't come here, Dr. Finley. There may be casualties. We are trying to do a head count, sir."

"Of course, I should come down."

"They won't let you in. Sit tight. I'll call you when we've assessed the situation. I have to go."

"Yes, yes. Of course."

He sat on the side of the bed, his heart still pounding. He was so close to retiring. He shuddered, wondering which of his employees might have been in the rehab room located in the basement of New York Medical Rehab. There could have been any number of patients and staff down there. It made him feel sick. What could have happened? Why now? They had prided themselves on their safety protocol. All sorts of checks and

Scared Truths

balances were in place. The building had been remodeled a few years ago. Surely someone would have noticed something during the months of reconstruction. Could it have been a bomb? But why? All he could do was wait.

Walter was right. They probably wouldn't let anyone else in until they were sure the building was safe. Dr. Finley wondered where they were taking his patients. He moved his frail body from the bed and walked to the kitchen. He set a teapot on the stove to fix a cup of English tea. Perhaps the television would reveal something. He sat down in his old rocker. Maybe if he hadn't been asleep, he would have heard something. His apartment was close enough for him to walk to NYM when he was younger. Nowadays, he had to arrange a ride.

~~~~

The first report came about an hour after Dr. Finley had been startled awake by Walter. It was a brief statement on the news. "There has been an explosion at New York Medical Rehab. There is one known casualty. Patients and staff are being evacuated. Stand by for a full report."

He rubbed his forehead and let out a long sigh. This was going to be a big mess for him and the staff. What the hell had happened? When the phone finally rang, he jumped and grabbed it.

"Hello, hello. Tell me something good."

"Dr. Finley, it's Jessica. I suppose you've heard."

"Yes. Walter called. Tell me. How bad is it?"

"I heard it's only the rehab room. The corner of the basement was blown apart. They suspect a gas pipe under the building."

"I thought we did away with the gas when we did the reconstruction."

"We did, but they say it had nothing to do with us. It was an old pipe running under the building. No one knows at this point why it exploded."

"Who was down there?" Dr. Finley asked.

"They transported one patient and one physical therapist to the hospital. There was one casualty."

"Do you know who it was?" He held his breath.

"It was Roger. One of the patients in a wheelchair; Roger Halve-something."

"Halvesord. Roger Halvesord. Oh, how sad. What about the other man—James? They were usually down there at the same time."

"I haven't heard anything else. They're making us all evacuate. He's probably the one they transported in the ambulance."

"Where are they sending the patients?"

"Several places. It will be a mess 'til we find out the details."

"Well, we'll figure it out. Who were the therapists? Do you know who was on duty?"

"No, not yet, but I heard they weren't seriously injured. They said one had maybe a broken nose. He had a pretty bad bleed when he walked out behind the two men on the stretchers."

He sighed again. It must have been the new male physical therapist. He would take it all in stride being post-military. "Oh, you saw him. Anything else I should know? I feel useless."

"Seriously, there's nothing we can do. They have control of our patients, and we are being told to leave. I have to go, Dr. Finley. It could have been worse. Walter said he'd call you later. He's helping check all the rooms."

"Tell him to get out of there. Let them do it."

"You know Walter."

"Yes, yes. He's a good man. Okay, Jessica. Thank you. Keep yourself safe. Get out of there. Go home."

~~~~

Roger and his therapist had been against the far wall working on his balance and coordination. He had been up in the stander and was finally settling back into his wheelchair. The therapist had walked across the room to get some equipment and left him sitting there alone.

James was working with the new male therapist on strength and coordination in his arms. He had progressed to feeding and almost completely dressing himself. He still had to use a wheelchair, but things were finally starting to happen for him. His therapist had also walked away for a moment to get a pair of small dumbbells when the blast occurred.

James started screaming, "Gas leak! Gas!" He knew right away it was gas because he could smell the foul egg odor. The blast threw him out of his wheelchair onto the floor. He ended up lying almost face to face with Roger, who was gasping for air. He tried to crawl toward him, but he couldn't get his body to move. He started screaming.

"Help! Help us! We need help over here."

The odor was getting stronger. "It's gas! It's going to blow again! Someone?"

Roger was moaning, his breathing becoming quick and short.

"Hang on, Roger. They're coming to help. Someone? Anyone?"

The therapist suddenly turned James over on his back. He was holding a bloody towel on his face and attempting to move James with one arm.

"Sorry, buddy. I got hit in the face by something. It's only my nose. I've called for help. They will be here soon."

James turned his head toward Roger. "Help him," James told the therapist. "He's bad."

Roger's breathing was shallow and his color was becoming ashen. A large puddle of blood began to seep out from under him. The therapist turned his attention to James.

"Well now, James, let's see what's going on here. Are you feeling any pain anywhere? James, can you hear me? Are you feeling any pain?"

A minute before, James had been giving him orders. Now, there was silence. He pushed the towel hard on his own face so he could look down at James. Shit, this guy was going ashen too. What the hell? He knew all too well the signs of internal injuries from a blast. He hoped this sucker wasn't bleeding out inside. God, two for two? What the hell was going on? Clearly, the force had either thrown James into something or the direct blast itself had caused the injuries.

"James, can you hear me? Answer me!" he said sternly.

He heard a faint moan. "That-a-boy. Come on back. Come on."

Nothing. He tried to look at Roger, but every time he put his head down, the blood would gush out of his nose. Son of a bitch. He needed IVs—something to give them a chance. He heard someone talking down the hall.

"We're down here!" he yelled. "In the rehab room! Keep coming!"

The other therapist and two firefighters came through the door. Two EMTs were right behind them.

"I went to get help."

"God, am I ever glad to see you. I didn't know what happened to you. I have two men down. The one over there is the worst. They both took a direct hit from the percussion. Roger looks like he's bleeding out."

"What about you? Looks like you've got a profuse bleed going," said one EMT.

"I've got this. Attend to them."

He snuck a look as they assessed the situation. The EMT shook his head after a quick check of Roger. He didn't have to say anything. The pool of blood had doubled in size.

"Something cut right into his femoral artery. He's almost gone," he whispered.

"This is James," said the therapist. "He was giving me orders one minute and slipping away the next. I suspect internal bleeding due to the overpressure of the blast."

The EMT nodded.

"How many tours did you do?"

He held up two fingers.

"Right there with you, man. War's a bitch."

More EMTs arrived with stretchers. They hurriedly put James and Roger on them and said, "We've all got to get out of here as fast as possible. They haven't figured out how to turn off the gas, yet. If there's no one else down here, we have to go now."

"These two should be it. What about the others upstairs? Everyone else okay? Everyone out?" The therapist's towel was completely drenched with blood.

"As far as I know, these are the only two who were injured, and you, of course. Let's get you out of here and I'll take a look at your nosebleed."

They hurried out, following the EMTs, and the stretchers up the hall. They struggled up the one flight of stairs and then out to the street. Ambulances, firefighters, and EMTs were everywhere.

CHAPTER 27

They were finishing breakfast with Iron Crow, Maggie, and all the ranch hands at the kitchen table. Zane leaned close, and asked Catherine if she wanted to get some fresh air. He had his jacket hanging on the back of Iron Crow's chair, and placed it loosely around her shoulders.

"You may need this," he suggested.

They walked around the perimeter of the house, looking at the remnants of the vegetable garden and the mountains.

"I figured you might need a break from all the chatter at the table," Zane said. "It's what happens on a ranch of this size."

"I never really thought about it," Catherine confessed. "It's definitely an entirely different way of life."

The sun was beginning to rise from behind the top of the ridge.

"This view is spectacular," she said. Zane reached out and grabbed her hand as they walked up the front steps and entered through the huge double doors into the great room.

"The aroma in the house is a different fragrance than I've ever experienced. It's so relaxing," Catherine said.

"My mother's sage and sweet grass smudging." Zane stuck his nose up in the air and took in a deep breath.

"It's wonderful. It smells like the wind, only it's inside," she said.

"Better than line-dried sheets," he teased.

Zane had missed the scenes and scents of the ranch. Nothing had been comparable in any of the places he had been over all those years he'd stayed away. There was something different about the place he had lived for the first eighteen years of his life.

"I guess," Zane said, "I took for granted how spectacular this place is. Wait until we go up into the mountains with Iron Crow. I can't wait to see your face."

"Okay, so you will be watching me while I'm taking it all in? I see." Catherine raised her eyebrows and stared at him with a grin.

"Exactly. You will see. You will see as you have never seen before."

~~~~~

Breakfast had been much the same as all the breakfasts—the ranch hands and Zane's family together every morning at the table. A few families had their own homes there, but anyone who lived in the bunkhouse or didn't want to eat alone came to the main house for meals. Zane's mother was finally allowing Maria to help her with the cooking and the cleanup.

Maggie was happy to have her son and his lovely Catherine there. She knew Iron Crow was especially excited this morning. He had big plans for a special ride for his future daughter-in-law. He was optimistic and had told her so. He wanted to take them to the place he and Maggie had called their own. It was a magical sacred place for them, and so it might be for Zane and Catherine.

Iron Crow had told the barn manager which horses he wanted tacked up, making sure Catherine would ride Maggie's favorite little mare. She was an aged mare and directly related to Zane's old pony, White Cloud. It would make a nice conversation for them.

Maggie watched Zane and Catherine as they chatted with each other and interacted with the men. It was such a shame they would live so far away. If only . . . but she had to be grateful he had finally come home. She knew full well she couldn't make things happen; she couldn't wish it so. She could only wait and see and pray. She would have to do even more smudging and praying while they were here.

She got up from the table and returned with a second bowl of biscuits and gravy. It was soon passed all around. She made sure there was no lack of sustenance for these men who worked so hard. She had always seen to that. Maria came in a few minutes later with a large bowl of fluffy scrambled eggs.

"God bless our hens," she said as she handed the bowl to Iron Crow.

"Yes, indeed," he said. "What would we do without our girls? Do you have fresh eggs on your farm, Catherine?"

"It's something I never really thought about. You know in my world they come in a box from the grocery store. I don't think about where they actually come from."

"Ah," said Iron Crow. "And that's what's wrong with most people today. They forget the work involved in the production." He was grinning.

Maggie was looking straight at her when Catherine looked up and said, "I forget how lucky we are to have eggs. It's a labor of love from our hens. It's a blessing they give us. Everything on this planet has a purpose. We sometimes forget we are all related. What we do, what they do, it all has an effect on us."

"I've taken a lot for granted," Catherine said. "I think we lose the true nature of ourselves when we live in the city. My little farm has taught me so much already."

"Well," said Iron Crow, "soon enough you will have your eyes opened by the big blue sky."

"I can't wait. I'm excited about the ride this morning."

"I hear he picked out a special horse for you," Zane said.

"Yep," Iron Crow said. "We brought her in last week."

Maggie watched as Catherine's expression changed. She spoke up, "He's teasing you. They did bring her up as soon as we knew you were coming. She's the horse I used to ride. She's an older mare and she will certainly take care of you. Don't let them scare you. She's only been out grazing."

Maggie smiled as the color returned to Catherine's face.

"We promise not to be too hard on you today, Catherine," Zane said and squeezed her hand.

~~~~~

The house was empty now. Everyone had scattered in their directions. Maria had asked if she could use the truck to go fetch groceries. It was a good day for that, and Maggie was happy to be totally alone in her house. She lit her bundle of sage and placed it in the smudging bowl. She slowly fanned the smoke toward herself with an eagle feather. She was determined to invite positive energy into the house for them.

Maggie hummed a smudging song her mother had taught her. In the early days, they had sung seven songs and smudged the different areas of the tipi. There were many ceremonies. Now there was no time for all that. Life was much busier. There was no time to sit and sing those songs. It was bittersweet. She had loved those days of simplicity, but she also loved this home, the ranch, and especially having her son home with his lovely Catherine.

There had been struggles in this house, but after Zane left, it seemed like Foster changed. He was more distant, but also kinder. Zane's leaving had been hard on all of them, but she knew it had been the hardest on him. He was an upstanding man in the community. Hardened by ranch life, he abhorred what he saw as weakness in others. He had been particularly tough on Zane. At least now, her son could pull all the pieces together and maybe forgive Foster and them for what they had done. It was the only way they could have had this outcome now. The ranch was their ranch, and when they were gone, it would be Zane's. She could only hope he still loved it enough to keep it. They had worried over what would become of their blessed land. She and Iron Crow felt they were stewards of its history and their heritage.

They had been working on a trust to protect it all from any development that would destroy or degrade the ranch, its livestock, and wildlife. They were hell-bent on defending their vision into the future. They wanted to be certain it could never become a toxic dump, clear-cut for timber, or used for mining. It would forever remain in the land trust, and continue to be a working ranch. It gave them both the peace of mind they needed, and satisfied their hearts. It also relieved Zane of any pressure to make decisions on their behalf or after they were gone. As long as he was alive, he would be the guardian of their land.

As she moved from room to room smudging, Maggie blessed what each room gave to them and the people that visited there. The house surrounded them with loving walls, and she was grateful for each of the memories. All negativity would be gone.

~~~~~

The three of them had ridden west with the sun behind them. The warmth felt soothing on Catherine's shoulders. Her hat was hanging down her back, held by the stampede string Zane had bought her. It was black and turquoise braided leather and had a piece of turquoise nugget on each strand. She loved it. She mused over what it must have been like riding out like this when Zane was a boy.

Maggie was right. The little mare was handy, yet easy to ride. She was smooth as glass and seemed to read Catherine's mind. The guys were being kind to her by riding at a steady but manageable pace. She felt a little uncomfortable when they headed down a slope since her legs weren't used to the pressure, but Zane had patiently adjusted her stirrup length and told her if her knees bothered her or her feet went to sleep to tell him as it meant he needed to readjust the length. So far, she was feeling no discomfort, only a little bit of fear at the degree of the downhill rides.

"We're almost there, Catherine," Iron Crow said. "We'll reach the plateau and then we can dismount and give our legs a break."

It was uncanny how Iron Crow read her almost as well as this little mare.

"Thank you, Parker. That would be nice. By the way, what's her name?"

"Whose name?" he asked softly.

"Oh, I'm sorry. This little horse. She's really quite remarkable. I like her a lot."

"Her name is Black Cloud. She's a direct descendant of the little mare Zane's pony White Cloud came out of."

"She certainly lives up to the Cloud part of her name. She moves as softly as a cloud. She's quite lovely."

"She was a remarkable horse for Maggie, but Maggie doesn't like to ride so much now. Her legs bother her. She says they get tired easily. She feels worn out."

"I noticed she's letting Maria help her in the kitchen. Are you sure she's okay?" Zane asked.

"She's been to the doctor. They say all her tests are normal. Face it; we're old!"

They had been slowly climbing and letting the horses pick their way up what seemed like quite a mountain to Catherine, and finally, they reached the most beautiful scene. The wind came up across the plains with the sweetest smell, and you could see across the mountain range looming before her. Catherine couldn't help herself. Tears started to flow down her cheeks and she couldn't say a word. They sat there in silence, the three of them still mounted on their horses, for quite a while.

Iron Crow dismounted in the smoothest move of a man coming off a horse Catherine had ever seen. He didn't even make a sound when his feet touched the ground. He reached over and took hold of Black Cloud's bridle, not that the mare even took a step while Catherine slowly dismounted. She wasn't a large horse, so Catherine easily reached solid ground. Zane had already dismounted and removed a canteen from his saddlebag.

"Here, Catherine. I'm sure you are parched."

She took several swallows and tried to hand it to Parker.

"No, thanks. I'm fine."

Zane took the canteen from her, swallowed a few sips, and returned it to his saddlebag.

"We can hobble them and tether them while we grab a bite, and then we have something to share with you, Catherine."

The two men hobbled and tethered the horses. Iron Crow handed them each their lunch from his saddlebags.

"Let's see what goodies Maggie and Maria cooked up for us."

They sat on the rocks, eating their lunch in silence. Catherine could not believe the view.

"This is like being inside a Steven Spielberg movie on the large screen. It's hard to comprehend the vastness of this space. It's graphically impressive."

"You are looking toward the Continental Divide, my dear," Iron Crow said. "Few people have been to this spot to see this exact view."

"I can't believe the strength of the wind up here," Catherine replied. "At times, when it takes my breath away, I can't even speak."

"There are Native stories told about these winds," said Iron Crow. "One of them happened not so long ago. A straight wind blew in and completely took down fifty-five acres of lodgepole pines. Laid them flat out like a steam roller had come over them. Many of the people kidded that Chicken Little was right after all. The sky was really falling, but it was really only the trees."

Zane chuckled. "Don't pay any attention to him and his stories. You should hear some of the things he told me when I was a kid, and I believed him."

"But this is a true story. You can—what do you call it—Google it when you get back to the house. And anyway, you were a little boy. You needed to be entertained."

Catherine was laughing.

"What are you laughing at?" Zane asked.

Scared Truths

"You two are so much alike. I can't imagine what went on when you were growing up."

"It was complicated," Iron Crow said. "But then there were times like this where he and I would slip away. Those were the moments we lived for. Now I get to share them with you both. Come, Catherine."

Iron Crow helped her to her feet and steadied her against a huge gust of wind.

"It's not far. It's a sacred place where Maggie and I would slip away to. It's protected from the wind."

Catherine carefully followed Iron Crow with Zane bringing up the rear. It took only about ten minutes to walk around the perimeter to the back side of the mountain. It was truly an even more spectacular view of the plains. A complete opposite of the mountain side, this was flat and expansive. There were small black dots down in the basin she couldn't quite make out.

"What are they?" she pointed.

"That's another part of our remuda of horses. We bring them up here in the summer. We are about ready to move them down to the low country for the winter months. It's much too harsh up here for them then. They will be moved to safer lower ground where we can tend to them."

"How do you keep them all together when you move them?"

"They have been doing this for years. They know. Each generation knows the routine. They pretty much know where the gates are, where we have to go."

"That's fascinating."

"Maggie and I used to come up here and spend hours on the back side of this mountain. And that's all I'm going to say about that, except as the mother goes, so goes the child," Iron Crow said softly.

Catherine had to ponder that.

"I'll leave you two up here while I go find some place to relieve my little pain."

As Iron Crow dipped out of sight, Zane took Catherine in his arms and faced her away from him, looking out at the grasslands.

"Do you see what I see?"

"Oh, my God, Zane, how could you have ever left here? It already has a strong hold on my heart. I mean I feel like it's in my soul. It's so heavy on my heart to look at it because in every direction there is so much natural beauty."

"They say the plains reach out to the horizon and then come back and get under your skin. Maybe that's what you are feeling. My mother used to say it reaches inward and wraps itself around your soul. Once Montana has a hold on your heart you will never be the same."

"Oh, Zane, it's beyond anything I could have imagined." She felt him sigh before she heard it.

She turned around and kissed him. It was another one of his kisses setting her on fire.

"Too bad we aren't alone up here on the back side of the mountain." He grinned.

They slowly walked back down to the tethered horses and found Parker sitting on a large rock facing out at the Great Divide. He had a flute in his hand, and he began to play when he heard them on the shale. Catherine felt her body shudder with the melodious tune he played. When his song was over, Iron Crow spoke in his native tongue, and then he turned and said to Catherine, "It's a Giving Thanks prayer to Creator. I thanked him for this place, this day, and the two of you."

"Thank you, Parker. Thank you very much."

She watched as Zane hugged his father, un-hobbled Catherine's little mare, and asked her, "Do you need me to fix your stirrups, Catherine?"

"No, I think they're fine."

He held her horse's bridle while she mounted up.

The two men swung easily from the ground into their saddles and they began the slow descent down the mountain. This time, Zane was in the lead, Catherine was in the middle, and Iron Crow brought up the rear. She wouldn't have missed these moments for anything, and now she could enjoy watching Zane and his horse pick their way down the slow decline.

CHAPTER 28

"Yes, yes, I do understand . . . . It's devastating. We had no indication there was anything to be concerned about . . . . I know, I know. Those pipes run under a lot of the buildings in New York. It was going to be bad no matter where it happened . . . . Yes, thank you."

Dr. Finley hung up the phone. John Phillip, Executive Administrator for NYM, had called to tell him they had temporarily shut down the rehab center until repairs were made to the basement and they were sure it was safe for employees to return. In the meantime, most of the facilities where their patients had been transported were utilizing the NYM employees to care for their added guests. It was the best solution for everyone.

Jessica was busy boxing up Dr. Finley's belongings, preparing him to move into her house. He hadn't needed much. His entire life had been devoted to others, especially after his wife died. The explosion was perplexing. Why at that moment? Why in that room? They had never given any thought to the dangers underneath the floor. Who would have? Now both of those two souls were gone. Together.

"Say, I'm going to need to contact the man with the government who called me recently about James and Roger. I should let him know what happened. Did you come across my telephone pad by the phone?"

"Yes. It's still right there on the counter. That's one of the last things I was planning to pack. You know, in case anyone called you."

Jessica handed the phone pad and telephone to him. He sat down and slowly dialed the phone. It rang four times before Bill Brannan answered.

"Mr. Brannan, this is Dr. Finley from New York Medical Rehab."

"Yes, sir. How are you doing today?"

"I'm fine, but I'm afraid I have some bad news for you concerning those two gentlemen you called about. There was a terrible explosion at our facility, and I'm afraid they were both killed."

"That's horrible. What happened?"

"There are old gas pipes running under our building. They weren't even supposed to be active. We don't know yet exactly what occurred, but Mr. Campbell and Mr. Halvesord were in the rehab fitness center in the basement at the time. Neither of them had a chance. They did not survive. It's been devastating for us."

"I'm sorry to hear this, of course. What terrible news. And I'm sorry about your facility."

"Yes, yes. They have us closed at the moment. Do you know if there are any next of kin? I mean we don't know who to contact."

"I'm sure I can help you with that. Let me do some research and I'll get back to you."

"Since you won't be able to reach me at NYM, let me have my friend give you my cellphone number." He handed the phone to Jessica. "Honey, tell him my number please."

Jessica gave Bill Brannan the information and handed the phone back to Dr. Finley. "He wants to say something else to you."

"Dr. Finley," Bill said, "please let me know if I can help in any way, and I'm sorry for the loss of these two men."

"Yes. Thank you. I'll wait to hear from you."

Dr. Finley was relieved and hopeful Bill Brannan would be able to shed some light on what they should do with the bodies. Currently, they were being held in refrigeration at the city morgue as part of the evidence of the blast. It would help expedite things when there was known next of kin. What a ghastly way their lives had ended.

~~~~~

Bill Brannan tossed his cellphone on his desk and sat down in his office chair, staring out the window. *What the hell?* he thought. He sure hoped an accident was the case, and it was simply an old ruptured pipe. *There's no other logical explanation. How could anyone plan an explosion for precisely the moment those two were down in the basement? No way that had happened. It had to be purely coincidental. But son of a bitch. Both of them dead at the same place at the same time?*

He picked up the phone and dialed Buck Matthews' number. *What a screwy turn of events. Well, at least now, I can retire without ever having to think about those two again. It's sort of closure. Holy shit.*

"Buck Matthews, how the hell are you?"

"Bill, hey, man. I'm fine. What's up with you?"

"I have some news for you. You aren't going to believe this. James and Roger are dead. It's nuts. They were both in the basement at the rehab center when a gas pipe blew. They were killed at the same place at the same time. How the hell screwed up is that?"

There was silence on the phone. "Buck, are you there, man?"

"Yes. I'm stunned. I mean, I really didn't like either one of those guys, but that's crazy. What the hell happened?"

"Dr. Finley called me from the rehab and said they still don't know exactly what caused the blast, but it was likely a gas pipe under their building. They are still in an active investigation. Meanwhile, they are searching for next of kin for these two."

"Well, have you talked to Zane?"

"Not yet. I wanted to see if you could give me any insight. You're the one who did the most research and followed the stories on them."

"As far as I know, Catherine is it for James. He came out of an orphanage into foster care. She was it for him. Roger? I'm not sure. You'd have more leads on that one than me. Maybe try his old office."

"Well, let me see what I can dig up."

"By the way, Bill," Buck said, "I'm in the process of moving."

"Moving?"

"Yeah, Deb, the kids, and I are moving back to my folks' ranch in Montana. It's time."

"Good for you. I have a few months here myself, and I'm done. Can't wait. Well, Buck, good luck to you. I'll be in touch. I'm sure this will bring closure for Catherine at last. But what a hell of a way to go."

"I know. Thanks, Bill, for everything."

~~~~~

Buck was sitting at the kitchen table with a cup of coffee in front of him when Deb came down from putting the twins to bed.

"Who was on the phone?"

"Bill Brannan. It seems Catherine's ex-husband is dead along with his buddy, Roger. They were both killed in an explosion."

"Oh, goodness."

"Remember I told you they both had serious brain injuries and were in the same rehab in New York City. Well, now I have to tell Catherine they are dead. I hope she'll be relieved."

"That's awful. When are you going to tell her?"

"No point in messing up tonight for them. I'll call in the morning. Bill was asking about next of kin. I think Catherine is it for James, and Bill's researching Roger. What a strange turn of events."

"Well, maybe they didn't suffer."

"Depends on how you define suffer. Their lives changed dramatically after the government got done with them. I'm glad this is going to be behind us."

"Me too. Can't wait to get settled and stop with this part of our lives."

"I agree."

He reached up, took her hand, and pulled her onto his lap.

"We have a lot to be grateful for. Can't wait to focus on us and the kids."

~~~~~

The investigation was leaning toward it simply being a terrible accident when the old gas pipe exploded. Work was being done on a nearby tunnel, and they suspected it was the cause. However, they were attempting to discover why the line had been active. Dr. Finley filed the appropriate documents releasing James Campbell's body to Catherine DeLong. The city morgue would handle contacting her.

It had been a task, but Jessica had tracked down Roger Halvesord's last employer, who had directed her to his former office manager, Eve Brodie. She had to enlist the help of a computer-savvy friend who gave them the current phone number of Eve, who had married, and was now Mrs. Evan Johnson. Eve agreed to accept the cremated remains of Roger. They turned the information over to the coroner and focused on Catherine DeLong.

"It seems strange this will be our final act as staff of NYM. We usually don't lose our patients, do we, Doc?" Jessica asked.

"No, we don't, and I hate to say it this way, but at least it wasn't anything we had any control over. We didn't fail them."

"No, we certainly didn't, and, honestly, in a way, it seems terrible to say, but they may both be better off this way. They died quickly."

"Yes, their recovery wasn't going to be remarkable, that was certain. They wouldn't have returned to their normal lives."

~~~~~

Zane had been in the barn early, spending time with Iron Crow. He rushed into the house with some of the ranch hands who were coming in for breakfast.

"Morning, Mom," he said as he kissed her on the cheek. "Has Catherine come down yet?"

"She was down after some tea. Buck called her."

"Oh?"

"I don't think it was a good call. She didn't say anything much to him, thanked him, and then she took her tea and went back upstairs. You should check on her."

"I'll go up right now."

He headed through the great room and vaulted up the staircase. He found her sitting on the edge of the bed staring out the window at the mountains.

"Morning, sweetheart."

When she turned to look at him, he could see she was crying.

"What happened? Tell me." He sat down on the bed next to her, tucked her under his arm, and pulled her close to him. "My mother said you had a telephone call from Buck. What is it? Did something happen to one of the horses, the dogs?"

She looked up at him and said, "Oh, no. Everyone on the farm is fine. It's James. He's dead. He and Roger are both dead."

"What happened?"

"Buck said he doesn't know all the details yet, but that Bill guy called him and said there was a gas explosion at the rehab center. They were both killed at the same time. I didn't think it would hit me like this."

"It's okay to feel something, Catherine. You had a history with him after all. You did love him."

"I know," she said softly, "but I wanted to be over him."

"You can't erase him. It's okay." He took a deep breath and pulled her even closer.

"In a way, I'm relieved. I hated thinking about him struggling. He was such an active man, always going, doing.

I couldn't imagine him in a wheelchair. It was not the kind of life he would want. This seems better for him. And Roger too. It had to be hard on both of them."

Zane handed her several tissues from a box on the nightstand.

"Thank you. I didn't expect this. I don't know what I wanted, but I don't think it was this. I wanted him to go away, but not like this. And Roger. I hated him, and now he's gone too. It feels strange. Buck was asking about next of kin. Zane, I'm the only one James had. He has no family. I think they are expecting me to make the decisions about him—you know, as far as funeral arrangements. I don't want to go through that again."

They sat in silence for a few minutes.

"Well, here's what you have to decide, Catherine. Do you need a funeral? Who would come? Anyone? I'm not saying this in a mean way, but maybe you should have him cremated."

"I don't know what he would have wanted. I don't even know if he told anyone what he wanted."

"Don't make it so hard on yourself. Maybe he had a will. Maybe it says what he wanted. Did he have a will when you were married to him?"

"Yes. I may even have a copy in my old paperwork. You know, I never really went through the stuff I brought when I moved to the farm."

"Well, I'm sure you could trust Mrs. Matthews if you wanted her to look for it, or we can look when we get back next week."

"Buck said they are holding his body for evidence right now. It's awful to think about him laying somewhere cold." Catherine inhaled deeply through her nose.

"I think it's standard procedure due to it being an accident, don't you? I mean, I'm sure the rehab needs to know what happened. It will be okay. Try not to think about that."

She took in a deep breath and exhaled slowly. Tears slid silently down her cheeks.

"I didn't expect this," she said. "I don't want it to ruin our time here. I think you're right. I'll call Effie and tell her where I think the box is. It's probably in the closet in my office. Okay, I'll take a few minutes to pull myself together and then I'll be down for breakfast. Go on down. I'm sure the men are already in, and I don't want you to miss time with them and your father."

"It's okay, Catherine. I'm here for as long as you need me."

"I'll be okay. I want to wash my face and freshen up a little."

Zane gave her a long loving hug and left her. He was relieved there was some finality to all of this at last. It was an awful outcome for James and Roger, but it would finally end Catherine's fears. Maybe now she could rest easier, knowing she wouldn't have to deal with either one of them ever again.

~~~~~

Zane grabbed a cup from the counter and poured himself some coffee. His mother was standing at the sink. He said quietly, "Catherine had some bad news. Her ex-husband and his friend, Roger, were both killed in a gas explosion in New York. She's upset, but she'll be down shortly."

"Oh, the poor dear. Is she okay?"

"It's been a long difficult time for her. She thought she'd already buried him once. Now this. It's tough on her. It's better that we're here."

Catherine walked into the kitchen from the great room, took her tea cup to the sink, and greeted Zane's mother.

"Good morning."

"Morning, dear. Can I fix you another cup of tea or coffee?"

"No. Thank you. I'll have juice at the table."

More ranch hands came in the back door. The conversation during breakfast had been the usual that morning. Men talking about the cattle, the horses, the chores to be done. Kidding about something that had happened the day before. Local news. Catherine was barely listening.

The men had gone, leaving Catherine, Zane, and Iron Crow at the table, and Marie busy in the kitchen. Zane's mother came to the table and stood behind Zane with her hands on his shoulders, rubbing them like she did when he was a young man.

"Maybe Catherine and I should take a little journey this morning," Maggie said. "I have something special I want to share with her."

Zane spoke up first.

"We rented the SUV so if you two wanted to go off together, it would be easy for you gals. I think today would be an excellent day to do that."

"I'll keep this guy out of your hair," Iron Crow told Catherine. "I'm sure I can find something to keep him occupied." He winked at Zane.

"What do you say, Catherine?" Zane asked. When Catherine didn't seem to hear him, he tried again. "Catherine, my mother thought maybe you'd like to get off the ranch today. Do you want to go?"

Catherine lifted her eyes from staring at the middle of the table.

"I think that sounds perfect. I'll get a wrap or jacket. The air seems a little chilly today." Catherine stood, stepped out from the long bench, and hurried out through the great room and upstairs.

"I'll take her up to Bynum. Even if we don't get out of the car, it will get her away for a while."

"I'll make sure she has her camera," Zane said. "Some of those old buildings and the view of the mountains should interest her. She has a keen eye." He kissed his mother on the cheek. "You'll be good for her."

"Ah, now, don't go getting all mushy on us," Iron Crow chided. "You and I have some horses to move. What say we gather up some men and go move the herd down? We should have started earlier, but we'll get it done. Why don't you girls find some place to eat or take a lunch? I'm sure Maria can handle lunch for the guys left behind. I'll pack us some stuff to take for today. Now go on."

He hugged Maggie as Catherine came back into the kitchen with a jacket draped over her arm. Zane kissed her, told her to have a nice time and not to forget her camera. He and Iron Crow headed out the back door.

~~~~~

"I think I left the camera out in the car. Did you want to take the SUV? I can drive," Catherine asked Maggie.

"I think that would be nice. Let me say something to Maria and I'll meet you out front. She's on the back porch fixing green beans. I'll be right there."

Catherine was sitting in the car when Maggie White Calf came out the front door with a beautiful red wrap around her shoulders. It made her dark hair look even richer. It was incredible how she only had gray streaks at her age—only a few wisps at her temples and a few scattered threads. Her complexion was flawless.

"Follow the ruts out of the yard and head toward the gate you can barely see the top of in the distance. It's going to be a perfectly clear day for your photos."

Catherine sat up straighter so she could see where to steer the car.

"I noticed quite a few pictures on your walls. They are excellent."

"Some of the boys who've lived here with us over the years were interested in photography. We tried to encourage their talents."

"I'm far from talented with my shots. I simply enjoy it for my own pleasure. I like what I see and want to capture it."

"You will have some nice views up in Bynum since some of the old buildings are interesting. There is old artwork on the sides of some of them."

They grew into silence. Finally, Catherine spoke.

Scared Truths

"I'm sorry. I wandered off. I had a little setback this morning and was thinking about something."

"It's fine. I like silence, and I don't get out this way as much anymore. I was enjoying the scenery."

Catherine was enjoying driving down the two-lane road with the mountains to the left, and north, and the open grasslands to the right. She took in a deep breath.

"I suppose Zane told you."

"He said you suffered a loss. I know a little about your situation. I don't need to pry."

"It's complicated. Before I met Zane, I was told my husband had been killed in a terrible car accident. We had a funeral. It was awful. Then, recently, I discovered James wasn't the victim in the wreck after all and was still alive. I'm trying to save you the details. Anyway, his decisions changed a lot of lives. I was getting used to the idea of his being alive when Zane told me he had nearly drowned and was in rehab in New York City with a brain injury. Now, today, they tell me he has really died in a gas explosion. And it's not only him. His college buddy, Roger, is dead too. It's a bit much."

"Well, I guess so. How dreadful. That's very disturbing."

Catherine thumped her fingers on the steering wheel, then turned the volume lower on the radio.

"I confess. Part of me is feeling a twinge of loss, but then another part of me is feeling relieved. It's all been like a bad dream."

"I'm sure it is."

"And, in fact, not so long ago I did have a sort of dream, and I swear, I didn't know if I was really dreaming or if I was seeing it. Right after that, I was sitting at the beach, and I thought I saw a man's body in a wave. He was struggling and trying to get to the surface, but there really wasn't anyone there. I sat searching for a while, but I never saw it again. Then, I was in a half-awake, half-asleep state one night and thought I was drowning or someone was drowning. There was a dolphin pushing me or a person up toward the surface, but I couldn't tell who the person was. It's surreal to think now maybe it was about him and not me at all."

"Has this sort of thing happened to you before?"

"Yes, do you mean did I have feelings or dreams about things—sort of premonitions? Yes, and I do know some people associate that with the devil or bad things."

"I'm sure you know about my people and our visions."

"Yes. In fact, Zane shared his experience in the cave with me. I wrote a story about him and a cat. I certainly believe we get messages, and I've read about Native American visions. I believe these things are possible."

"Sometimes it's hard to ascertain the meaning of the messages. Sometimes we simply know, and other times we have to wait."

Catherine turned and glanced at Maggie. "I do get that. In a way, I wanted James to go away, and I never liked his friend, Roger, but I hadn't gone to the point where I wanted either one of them dead."

"These events are nothing you could have expected or changed. Isn't it a matter of bad fate for them to be in the wrong place at the wrong time?"

"Or maybe karma? Maybe things caught up with them."

"We will never know, will we?"

"That's true. Now I'm expected to make a decision about what to do with his body. He has no family. It's convoluted. I'm not technically married to him, since I have a death certificate but yet . . . ."

"I see what you mean. It is complicated."

"Zane suggested I have James cremated, since no one would be likely to come to a funeral anyway, since anyone who knew him as James DeLong already believes he's dead."

"But then that's a solution."

"I think that's what I have to do. It makes it easier. Buck said they are holding his body as part of the evidence for the investigation. It makes me queasy to think about him in a refrigerator."

"Well, now, maybe we can focus on our little trip and put this subject away for a while. Stick it in a pretty little flowered box up on a shelf in an imaginary closet."

Catherine started to laugh, and then Maggie started to laugh with her. Tears of relief slid down Catherine's face.

"Thank you," Catherine said.

"For what?"

"For allowing me to laugh at a terrible situation. I needed this. And by the way, you have an infectious laugh."

"It's how I got through some terrible situations myself. Sometimes I would force myself to laugh because if I didn't, I would cry. I don't like to cry."

"I know what you mean. How far is this little town we are heading to?"

"It's there, up the road aways. I don't really know how far, but we will know when we get there."

Catherine and Maggie looked at each other and began to giggle. It would be a pleasant day of enjoying the scenery, taking pictures and forgetting about everything else.

CHAPTER 29

Zane and Catherine had only a few days remaining with his parents. The four of them were sitting at the kitchen table talking about old times when the phone rang. Zane got up and answered it.

"Yes, sir, she's right here. Hold a moment."

He pointed the phone at Catherine.

"It's the coroner. He needs to talk directly to you."

Zane watched Catherine as her shoulders sank and she leaned on the counter.

"Yes, I understand. Please have them contact me directly at this number." She slowly placed the receiver back on the wall phone. "He's going to have a funeral home call me." She leaned against the counter, waiting. In a few minutes, the phone rang again.

"Yes, yes. Cremation. No. Is there another option? Then can I get back to you on that?" She wrote down and then repeated a phone number. "Of course. I'll call you before then. Thank you."

Zane didn't know if he should grab her or let her be. She walked back across the kitchen and sat down.

"The authorities released his body. They want to know if I want his cremains."

Catherine turned facing Zane. He tenderly flicked a tear off her cheek.

"Zane, I don't think I want them. What would I do with him? I don't really want him at the farm. Is it awful to feel like that?"

Scared Truths

Zane hesitated and his mother spoke up.

"Did they offer you another solution?"

"They asked me if I wanted him mailed to me and I said 'No,' and they said they could hold him with other cremains, and once a year, they take them out to sea. They have a priest go with them to bless the ashes and then they dump them overboard. I told them I'd get back to them. What should I do?"

Zane gently pushed Catherine's hair behind her ear and wiped another tear from her cheek. "Honey, you don't have to decide right now. You can think about it."

"It's terrible to think he was in the ocean when he nearly drowned and I might throw him back in the thing that killed him. Doesn't that seem terrible?"

"What else would you do with him?"

"I hate to say it, but if I knew where she was, I'd send him to Arianne."

Zane let out a little chuckle and said, "Well, I bet I could enlist someone to find her for you."

"I'm not sure I was being serious," Catherine said half-heartedly.

"No, but that's not such a bad idea."

"No. It would be awful. I think I'll let them do the ocean disposal. Does it really matter? It's being paid for by either NYM or James' funds. I'm not sure."

Iron Crow spoke up. "His spirit is already gone. The body is only a vessel for our journey. I don't know if that helps you at all."

"Yes, I think it does. It's only ashes. It's not really him. Then, it will finally be over. At least it will be over for him."

Maggie got up and pulled tissues from a box on the counter and handed them over Catherine's shoulder. She lingered behind her.

"It's an answer and an end to the vision you had at least," Maggie said. She patted Catherine's shoulders and sat back down. There they all sat quietly. Iron Crow finally broke the silence.

"Don't you think it's a perfect afternoon to take a spin around the ranch? We only have a few days left, or so I've been told."

Zane had been avoiding setting a date to leave.

"We can take our rental car," Zane said, hoping his mother would join them.

"I'll get my wrap," his mother said. "The one you bought me so long ago." She patted Catherine's shoulder as she walked behind her. "I'm glad this story has an ending for you two. It will be a good day to be outside."

~~~~

The return date on their airline tickets was open, but Catherine knew their days at the ranch were coming to an end. She was anxious to get back to some form of normalcy, and to see her dogs and horses. She had awakened in time to enjoy the early rays of sunlight playing through the thin curtains in their room. Zane hadn't stirred yet, so she lay quietly waiting and trying not to think about anything at all. When he finally moved and opened his eyes, she was facing him and smiled.

"Good morning."

"Morning to you. What time is it?"

"I don't really know. First light is hitting the curtains."

Zane sighed and stretched.

"Is there anything you'd like to do today?"

Catherine studied his face—his chiseled jaw, the perfect nose, his soft brows, his smooth skin. He was such a handsome man.

"I don't want to pressure you, but could we decide when we are going to leave? I'd like to make sure Effie and Roan are okay with the timing of our return."

"Do you want to call them now? I mean, I understand you want to get home, but it means we are kind of kicking them out."

"Sure, we can do that. I'll call them after breakfast. Are you going out with Parker today?"

"Yes, I think I'll take advantage of every chance I can to spend time with him."

"Then I will spend time with your mother and Maria. I want to get some of their recipes and hang out here at the house."

"It works for me. Feeling a little tired, are you?"

"Yes, this thing with James and Roger zapped me."

"Understandable. At least now you have some sort of closure. It's terrible to say it this way, but he is finally gone, and Roger too."

"It's sad and it's better for them at the same time."

Zane reached up and touched her face. She pushed her chin down in his hand.

"You have been so good to me," Catherine said softly. "Thank you for your patience with all of this."

"What else could I have done? I love you. Thank you for coming to Montana with me. It has meant everything."

"I'm glad I came. I love your mother. She's such a kind and gentle person, and what can I say about Iron Crow? He's quite unique and likeable."

"Yes, he certainly is."

"Well, don't they say the apple doesn't fall far from the tree? Now I know where you get some of your mannerisms and certainly your dry wit."

"It's Native American humor. Iron Crow would zing me with some of his quips and it's only now I'm understanding and appreciating some of the things that were said. In a way, I wish I had known he was my father, and yet, in another way, I can understand the roles they had to play. Life certainly has its twists and turns."

"Yes, you're right about that." She kissed him. "I want to freshen up."

Catherine turned away from him, tossing the covers off and rolling out of bed. "I'll only be a minute. If you want to wait, I'll be right back."

"I'll be right here," he said with a smile.

~~~~~

It was another perfect day. Iron Crow drove them around the ranch, telling stories as he recalled his time with Zane and things that had happened after Zane's abrupt departure. It moved her heart hearing him tell of things he had longed to share with his son.

Catherine's mind drifted back to how she had felt when she and Zane started driving across the plains.

"The Blackfeet tried to get along with the strange new people who came into our peaceful world," Maggie said.

Catherine was startled. *How did Maggie know what she was thinking?* She picked up her sunken shoulders and sat up taller in her seat. She hadn't realized she had slumped down into the corner.

Maggie continued. "The elders told me the Blackfeet were shocked when we saw the first cattle. Those creatures smelled terrible, and we couldn't understand how they could eat such a thing. The strange white settlers smelled as well. Their layers of clothing were often filthy dirty, and they hardly ever bathed in the river, or gave their bodies a chance to breathe."

"I never thought about what a shock it must have been to have the strangers come and take away everything that had been yours," said Catherine. "It must have been difficult to watch the destruction of everything the Native Americans had known and respected."

"We only took what we needed, but they ravaged everything. They killed for the sport of killing. They didn't even respect their own possessions. They left things along the trails and didn't care what they destroyed in their journeys."

"It had to be heartbreaking."

"In the beginning, we tried to understand and help them, but they were not interested in our ways. They thought we were ignorant and heathens. They had no idea how in touch we were with nature, the rhythms of the seasons, or how to live off the land without destroying it. Today, you see the results of their destruction and disrespect. At least we saved some of it through our reservations and our ranches."

"I can't begin to comprehend it all." Catherine sighed.

"Take us to the river, Zane, so we can walk and listen to its song. It will refresh us and remind us of a better day."

~~~~~

Catherine took in a deep breath and reached into the water to retrieve a pale turquoise stone. It suddenly slipped from her hand and fell back into the water. When she tried to pick it up again, she discovered it had split right down the middle. She held the two pieces in the palm of her hand and showed them to Maggie. Maggie took them from her and held each piece separately, then put them back together.

"This reminds me of the Blackfeet Nation. We were once strong and solid like this rock. Then the white men came from the East and tore us apart. You can hold the two pieces together, but the stone and the people will never be the same."

She handed the two pieces back to Catherine. Maggie hummed as they all walked along the riverbank. She and Catherine stopped to sit on the rocks in the sunlight. Zane and Iron Crow continued their walk, heading up the rise to the truck.

Zane's mother told her tales of another life. Catherine could picture the children splashing in the river while their mothers laughed and enjoyed the pleasantries of simpler times. It made her sad to think about how much the world had changed in such a short period of time.

Maggie told her the story about White Buffalo Calf Woman, who was sent to bring the people back to the Creator. She also talked about how the government recognized the Native Americans' strong relationship with the buffalo.

"They figured if they killed the herds, the tribes would be forced to surrender their lands and become a 'civilized people.' The military was ordered to kill the buffalo to deny them food, clothing, and all the things the animal provided. They believed they could do more harm by hiring buffalo hunters than by using the army."

Catherine could feel Maggie's distress as she watched her wring her hands, and she saw them shake as Maggie settled them in her lap.

"I was told when the great iron giant came across the plains, the world changed for us. The railroads allowed the slaughter of thousands of buffalo. Thousands of the buffalo were killed for food for the people building the railroad, but after it was built, they were killed because they were in the way of the trains. Sometimes their numbers were so vast they pushed the trains off the tracks. They killed them just to kill them."

Maggie sighed and pushed a strand of hair behind her ear.

"I can't even imagine the pain this must have caused the people who had relied on the buffalo for so much." Catherine took Maggie's hand in hers and held it.

"The traders and trappers killed them for their hides, leaving the rest of the animal to rot. It was devastating for our people to watch. Over one and a half million hides were sent by train to the east. The elders still tell stories of the bones piled high."

"I haven't done enough research to understand all this, but it hurts my heart, and it makes me even sadder than I was when Zane drove me toward your house."

"It was worse for us than the buffalo. By the turn of the century, the Native American population was only 237,000. There had been over one million of us living here on Turtle Island before the white man came. It was a dark time for my people."

"I didn't know. They don't teach us these things. I had no idea this trip would impact me in this way. When I was in elementary school, I drew a picture of an Indian chief in full headdress. I don't even know how I did it. It came rushing out of me."

"Catherine, you have us in your soul. Our blood runs through you. You know, our children always come home to their people."

"But that's the hard part, Maggie. I don't really know much about my ancestors. No one talked about it. No one in my family said anything about it—not until I was taking care of my Uncle Walton. He told me. That's when things began to make sense to me. I had always felt so connected to nature, and it didn't seem like others felt it to the depth I did. It was disturbing to feel—well, isolated. As if my feelings were so exclusive to me and no one else got it."

"I can understand that. It was difficult for our children when they took them and sent them east to be what they called 'educated in the ways of the white people.' Many of them tried to run away and come home. It was heartbreaking for the families as well as those children. They had no choice. Many of our children did not survive. They took most of them to Carlisle, Pennsylvania and other places. Families never knew what happened to their children."

"I have wondered if my grandmother was taken there, and if that's why I was born in Pennsylvania."

"You will have to ask."

"I'm afraid there isn't anyone to ask who is living now except my mother, and I'm not sure she cared to find out this kind of information. She divorced my father when I was about to become a teenager. Our lives were pretty much removed from that part of my family afterwards."

"Oh, I'm sorry."

"Yes, thank you. My mother made decisions she thought were the best for all of us, and my stepfather did provide a very solid life for us."

"Well, that's something."

"Yes, it is, and she did love and take care of us."

Iron Crow called out, interrupting them, motioning for them to come up the hill.

"Come, ladies. It's time to head back to the house. I'm sure Maria will be wondering who is going to pare the tub of potatoes."

"I was up early and did them already, and you know it! Stop teasing me, you silly man."

She took Catherine's hand as they climbed together up the slope to the truck and joined the men.

~~~~~

Dinner had been delicious with venison stew and all the fixings. The ranch hands had wandered off after dinner one by one. Catherine, Zane and his parents sat later than usual in the living room talking about the day's events. They decided to ride out in the morning for one last time before it was time to say goodbye. It was bittersweet for Catherine knowing soon she and Zane would be heading back to Florida.

Maggie rose quietly and went to a small table in a corner of the great room. She came back to Catherine and laid a map of Montana on her lap. She then handed her a string with a sewing needle dangling from it.

"Hold this needle by the thread over the map anywhere you would like. Don't think too much about it. Hold it still and breathe in a normal rhythm."

Suddenly, the needle began to move in a circular pattern. Round and round it swung, and then just as it had started, it stopped.

"You are connected to whatever place is under the point of the needle," Maggie said.

Catherine carefully held the needle in place and Zane leaned over and said, "Kiowa. The needle is over Kiowa."

"That's good place. Good energy. Bear medicine. Black bear. Grizzly." Iron Crow continued, "Brings healing, renewal, and rebirth."

"Well, I certainly can use all of those," Catherine said, as she covered her mouth and yawned. "I think I'm going to turn in. Thank you so much for a remarkable day."

"I'll be up in a minute, Catherine." Zane lingered a little longer with his parents.

Catherine took a long hot shower and put on a flannel nightgown, as the nights had been quite cool. When she walked into the bedroom, she was happy to see Zane already in bed. She curled into the warmth of his body. He was almost asleep, but he turned to gather her into his arms, and kissed her on the neck.

"Thank you, Zane, for insisting that I come out here with you. I know I was resisting, but you were right. I'm glad I got to meet your parents, and to see why this place means so much to you. It has definitely impacted me."

CHAPTER 30

She slid out of bed before daybreak. Catherine was glad she had managed to get away without disturbing Zane. She dressed in the darkness, luckily remembering she had piled her clothes in a heap on the hamper the night before. She quietly snuck out the bedroom door, and tiptoed down the stairs, only stopping briefly at the front door to pull on her boots. She headed across the great room and through the kitchen. She was relieved that, miraculously, no one was there.

Catherine headed straight to the barn and almost ran into one of the ranch hands in the semi-darkness. He tipped his hat to her.

"I wanted to go for a quick ride before breakfast. I need the little paint horse. The black and white one."

He didn't question her, simply tacked up the horse and gave her a leg up, and off she went. He called out to her as she trotted away.

"Did you want me to tell someone where you're headed?"

"I'm not going to go far. I'll keep the house at my back so I don't get lost!" she called over her shoulder.

Heading toward the mountain, they kept a steady pace. Catherine had had a fitful night of tossing and turning. She had seen James' car careening off the mountain and bursting into flames. Feeling the panic of her heart beating out of her chest, she had stood in front of his casket, looking at what was unrecognizable. Roger had come out of nowhere and was reaching, grabbing at her. He had pinned her up against a wall and tried to kiss her.

After awakening several times, she'd drifted back to sleep, only to begin the dreams again. She saw two men sitting in wheelchairs. She had been fighting in the sea, trying to swim to the surface. When she decided to get out of bed, she had been drenched in sweat. Zane barely stirred as she snuck silently away.

It felt refreshing to have the crisp air in her face and the horse beneath her. It seemed like the little horse was much more eager to go than it had been the other day. Catherine was holding it back. Pink rays streaked the sky as the sun rose behind her. It was getting easier for her to see the footing. She tried to relax and sit deeper in the saddle, but ended up posting or balanced in the stirrups because the horse had such energy.

Once they had been steadily trotting for a while, Catherine was able to slow to a walk and they settled in. Lost in her thoughts, she wondered what had brought so much drama to her dreams. Was it hearing the sad stories Maggie told, or was it the struggles she had been facing for what seemed an endless time?

The terrain was changing and they were approaching an incline when Catherine looked over her shoulder at the house. Her horse picked its way through a rocky area, giving her some confidence, and she let out a little rein. She liked the way it used its ears and was light in her hand. The horse was trained to neck rein and responded immediately.

Catherine didn't know how long she had been riding heading straight up, but she hit a flat spot and turned the horse around to once again look at the house. She gasped when she realized the house was nowhere to be seen. She took in a deep breath. She could have sworn she had ridden a straight-line west from the barn.

That's when she heard what sounded like a woman scream. She felt her horse flinch underneath her as she was thrown back in the saddle by the speed of a huge spook to the left. She suddenly felt the horse go down underneath her as they started sliding down the shale. She grabbed the saddle horn, trying to steady herself, but it was no use. Her left stirrup was already off her boot and her foot slid out of the right as she careened off the horse, holding tightly to the reins.

It happened so fast it knocked the breath out of her. She managed to slowly stand up in the dust caused by the slide and look down at the horse. It was in a sitting position and was shaking its head up and down. She was worried they would slide farther down the incline, but she knew she had to get the horse back up. She gently pulled on the reins and the horse leaned forward and tried to stand. On the second try it stood and shook like a dog shaking off water. Dust flew all around them. She was holding her breath. She slowly pulled on the reins again, and the horse tried to come up to her. Catherine soon realized there was a problem with one of its rear legs. It was holding it up, barely putting any weight on the toe. Once they were back up on the flat area, she moved to the side to check its leg. A good-sized notch was missing above its hoof on the outside, where it was dripping blood. The horse must have fallen with all its weight on it, and the shale had made the cut. There wasn't room to turn around at that spot, so Catherine had no choice but to walk farther up the trail. What had scared her horse? She was forced to walk slowly as it limped behind her. What a fine mess she'd gotten herself into. At least the sun was up and the morning light would help her get her bearings. Meanwhile, ranch hands would be about the business of the ranch, and soon Zane would realize she was gone.

Catherine hit a plateau and could see the mesa far below. A huge storm with dark clouds was on the horizon to the west. She knew how fast storms traveled across the mountains. Maybe it would move north and she would be okay. A lightning strike lit up the distant sky. She sighed; the thought of being stuck on the mountain in a thunderstorm was frightening.

Suddenly, the screaming sound happened again and her horse pulled back, ripping the reins out of her hand. She tried

Scared Truths

to hang on, but the force was too much. It pulled away and fled in a flurry of flying dust and stone. Catherine stood frozen. Now what would she do alone on the mountain?

Small stones began to pelt her from above; she turned, shielding her eyes from the sunlight. Above her on a stone ledge stood a mountain lion. There was nowhere for her to go. Her heart was beating in her chest so hard she could hear it inside her ears. She tried not to panic. She knew not to run. That's when the cat blinked at her and nodded its head. It turned and disappeared. Catherine knew she had to get off the mountain, but the storm was coming in rapidly.

Something moved to the left of her, and suddenly, there was the cat. The fear in her made her feel like she was going to pass out. The cat stood staring quietly at her, and then it turned and started walking up the trail. It stopped and looked back at her. Catherine thought for a minute it might be beckoning her. Could it be? Was the cat telling her to follow it? When she cautiously took a few steps toward the cat, it began to walk up the trail again. Catherine carefully followed. How could this be happening?

It didn't take Catherine and the mountain lion long to move around the ridge, and then Catherine realized where she was. It was the cave Zane had told her about—the cave he had found as a boy. The cat moved into the dark opening as the sky became dark, the winds picked up, and the rainy mist began. Catherine knew within minutes the full force of the huge black clouds would overtake them. She followed the cat into the cave.

This felt crazy. What if the cat attacked her? Who would ever find her in there? But the lightning and the cold pelting rain weren't an answer either. She knew the rain would wash away any hope of anyone seeing her footprints. As her eyes became accustomed to the cave's darkness, she heard something. The cat was lying on her side, and three kittens were nursing. This was surreal. Most mother cats wouldn't want a human anywhere near them, especially with their cubs. People had been killed by these big cats.

If only she'd had matches in her pocket, a flashlight, anything. She found a spot near the entrance of the cave, but out of the weather. The stone ledge above the cave kept the rain from coming in. The large cat ignored her as she licked her young.

Catherine had been sitting in the same position afraid to stir and her legs were cramping. She slowly, cautiously moved to a spot where she could stretch out, zipped her jacket up to her chin, and folded her arms to warm herself. The rain and the storm had caused the temperature to drop. She had drifted off to sleep, but she was suddenly startled awake when something touched her. Standing in front of her was a young man with his hand outstretched. She realized it was a Native American warrior. He had the top half of his face painted red, the bottom half was black, and there was a white circle around his mouth. He had black bear fur around his face, and the buffalo horns at the side of his head were turned down with the points ending at either side of his chin. Catherine was terrified, but she also wanted to reach out to him. There was something oddly familiar.

The young man was speaking to her, but she didn't understand his words. She took his hand and he helped her to her feet. He nodded at the cat and motioned for Catherine to move toward the mouth of the cave. Outside under the ledge stood the most beautiful red and white paint horse Catherine had ever seen. It had large feathers braided into its mane and a red ring painted around one eye. The warrior motioned to her, gave her a leg up on the horse, and silently began leading the horse down the mountain. Catherine felt like she was in an unreal world. She wanted to allow herself to be in the moment, yet she felt like she was in a dream, experiencing a time of long ago.

~~~~~

Scared Truths

Catherine could hear voices speaking quietly, but she didn't quite know where she was. She tried to open her eyes. The last thing she remembered was riding a horse out of the ranch early that morning. She had been upset about the dreams and all the things spinning in her mind. All she'd wanted was to get away from everyone and everything for a little while. She blinked several times and opened her eyes while trying to sit up.

"Hey, beautiful. Welcome back. Easy does it."

She looked into Zane's eyes.

"Welcome back? What are you talking about?" Her mouth was dry, and the words came off her lips thick and with some difficulty.

"Well, honey, you took a little spill."

Catherine tipped her head to the right a little and continued looking into his face. Her ear was ringing, and her head felt like it weighed a hundred pounds.

"What are you talking about? I didn't get hurt. My horse did, and then it got spooked, and I was left up on the mountain."

She knew someone else was in the room and heard the familiar chuckle of Zane's dad.

"Must have been something in the tea you drank last night," he chided.

"I don't understand."

Maggie hurriedly walked across the room and took Catherine's hand. "You gave us quite a scare. You've been out for a little while."

"What do you mean? I'm so confused." Catherine rubbed her forehead, and that's when she felt the bump.

"The ranch hand gave you a young gelding instead of my mother's mare," said Zane. "You must have thought it was the same horse. It was no one's fault. I don't know what you were thinking, going off alone. You barely got out of the yard. We think he must have stepped in a prairie dog hole and the two of you went down. That's when you bumped your head."

"I don't understand. I rode up to the mountain, and then we went down on the shale when a mountain lion came. The horse fell down and hurt its leg. I tried to go up farther so we could safely turn around. That's when the cat came back and scared the horse. I couldn't hold onto it and it ran away. Did you find it?"

"It's okay, Catherine," Maggie spoke up. "You don't have to talk now. We can talk about this later. You need to rest. You may have a slight concussion. I'll bring you some tea."

"Make it plain tea this time, Mother!" Zane glared at her.

Maggie squeezed Zane's arm before she walked out of the bedroom, pulling Iron Crow with her. Zane sat on the side of the bed. He leaned down, hugged Catherine, and kissed her on the cheek.

"I'm so glad to have you back," he said. "I wanted to take you to the hospital, but they said to give you a little time. My mother used an herbal compress to bring you back around. You scared me to death."

"I don't understand. Zane, I know I was up on the mountain. The cat came back and I was scared, but I wasn't scared. There was this terrible storm. I was more afraid of the lightning. The mountain lion, it came and it took me to the cave. Your cave, Zane. There were three little babies, and it took care of them right in front of me. I think I eventually fell asleep. That's when he came and got me."

"Who came and got you?"

"The warrior . . . the one you told me you saw. The one who came to you in your cave. He put his hand out and helped me up and talked to me in a strange language. He spoke to the mountain lion, and she nodded her head at him. Then he took me out of the cave. He had the most beautiful red and white paint horse I have ever seen. I rode her. He put me on his horse, I swear."

"I don't know what to say, Catherine. We can talk about this later."

"It's all so confusing. Was it you who came and found me? It was you, wasn't it? Were you the man in the cave?"

"It's okay. Don't get upset."

Before Catherine could say anything else, Maggie came into the room with a tray for her. She poured her a cup of tea and fixed it exactly the way she knew she liked it. Catherine sipped the warmth, letting it slowly slide down her throat. She tried to take it all in. The warrior in the cave had looked like Zane in a strange way, and what had happened seemed eerily familiar.

"I'll go now and leave you two alone."

Maggie hurried out the door as Zane called after her.

"And when you have a minute, Mother, you and I need to have a little chat."

~~~~~

Catherine had a terrible headache, and the bump on her head lasted a day or two. Zane wanted to rush her to the hospital to be sure she was okay, but she insisted she was fine. Now, too soon, they'd be leaving his mother and father and heading back to Great Falls and a flight home. She knew it was tough for Zane. There was no possibility they could stay any longer since Buck and Deb had been to Montana and were planning to permanently move to the Matthews' ranch. Catherine was getting dressed to go downstairs when Zane came to check on her. He found her standing at the window looking at the mountains. She turned to face him.

"Zane, tell me the truth. Were you the one who found the mountain lion? You didn't make up that whole thing, did you? I called him Charging Bear in the story I wrote, but his mother called him Cha Chu Nee. It connects with the bear medicine Iron Crow talked about and Kiowa."

"Yes, it does. It happened the summer Foster sold White Cloud. My mother sent me away for a while to her family. I think it was partly so I could learn their ways, but also to get me away from Foster and the pain I was feeling. My grandfather, her father, prepared me for a vision quest. He taught me ceremonies and tribal lessons. When I got back home, that's when the whole thing happened with the cat and the cave."

"Then it is true? You did nurse him back to health? And did you come and save me—you and the cat?"

"That's something you'll have to discover. Was it real? Was it a dream? Should I spoil the mystery of it all?"

"Stop it. That's not fair. You sound like Iron Crow. Think about it. Do you see how it has all come together like a woven tapestry? It amazes me how everyone's life has changed, and yet we are all still together. I'm happy for the Matthews. All of them are coming to their ranch. Effie said Roan is beyond excited. It's a dream come true having Buck and his family all be together. I'm excited for them too."

"Yes. It's truly moving to see how much Buck's life has changed. It makes all those years we spent away from home sort of melt away. When he got shot, it really put things in perspective for us. I never imagined him with kids, but it turns out he's become a heck of a father."

"You would have been one too, you know," Catherine said. "You have such a caring heart."

"I'm not sure I was cut out for that. I'm much better at tending to animals. Don't have the patience required for kids. Besides, I'm absolutely happy with the way things turned out for us."

"This trip did shift my thinking, Zane, and now we get to go back to Highberry. I can't wait to get settled again in our home."

"Yes, it is bittersweet. But hearing you say 'our home' makes up for it."

"Well, since we have Lauren to help out, I don't see why we can't become frequent visitors to Montana. Do you?"

She put her arms around him and hugged him.

"This makes me happy, Catherine. You have no idea," said Zane.

"Yes, I think I do know. I adore your parents. Your mother is remarkable, and I want to talk to her about her ancestry and her beliefs. She's a strong woman. And Iron Crow, what can I say? He is beyond unique. I love them both."

Scared Truths

"You do know they love you, don't you? You have been through a lot, and they think you are totally remarkable too."

"And so have you. Maybe now it's time for us to finally be. That's something I've always wanted. I don't have to be afraid of what is going to happen next. It feels sad about James and Roger, but at the same time, I know neither of them would have wanted to live their lives like that. It's over for them, and I'm finally really free to move on."

"I'm glad to hear this. I was worried it would drag you down."

Catherine thought about it for a moment and said, "In my other world, it would have, but your mother reminded me we only have today to count on. All the past days have been spent. The future days are there for us to dream about, and I'm not going to tell you yet, but I have a pretty big dream for next summer."

"Hey, now you're not being fair. You can't dangle that in front of me and then pull it away."

"You'll see. It will be well worth waiting for."

Catherine kissed him tenderly and took his hand as they walked down the beautiful wooden stairs he had walked or run down as a boy. She stopped him at the bottom of the steps.

"I can picture you as a little boy, running around this great room and your mother sitting there, doing her beadwork, watching you. I see Foster sitting there tentatively, taking it all in. He must have had some sense of who you would become. And then there is Iron Crow on the periphery, wishing it was him sitting in the great room. Fast forward and here we all are today. It's the way it was meant to unfold. We can't go back and change a thing. What matters now is how we all came together to be here in this moment. I want to live for that, Zane."

His mother came out of the kitchen and stopped abruptly when she saw them standing there in each other's arms.

"Well, what are you two up to this morning?"

"Dreaming," Catherine replied. "I'm dreaming about this man and this house and how it must have been."

"Ah, yes. This room has seen amazing things, and now it sees you two."

Iron Crow came through the kitchen door in a hurry and stopped short when he saw the three of them.

"Did I miss anything?" he asked.

"Not so much," Zane said. "We just came down."

"Well, I have some news. That pretty little mare you rode, Catherine, well her daughter is about to give us a late foal. I wanted to come get you, if you want to come out to the barn. We usually let them foal on their own, but she was having a little trouble."

Catherine giggled. It would be the perfect day. She was letting go of one life and a new one was about to begin.

"I can't think of a better way to end our visit. Zane, this is so exciting for me."

"You go with Iron Crow. I want to spend a little time here with my mother. I'll come out to the barn soon."

He kissed her tenderly, and Catherine and Iron Crow headed through the kitchen and out the back door.

"Well now, that's good for her. She's wanted to have a little breeding operation, so we will see what she thinks of this."

"She's a fine woman, Zane. You have done well finding her."

"Yes, I know. It's been interesting, this circle we've been in. She's come through a lot. She reminds me often of you. You're both strong women."

"God doesn't give us more than we can bear."

"That's not true and you know it. He's certainly given you your fair share."

"Yes, but I'm still here."

"You are only here because of your strength and will."

"And my faith in the process. This place is sacred to me. This land has a lot of history for our people."

"I know. Catherine wants to come often, and that's great for all of us. It will be nice to visit with Buck and his family as well. Never expected that either."

"I know. It certainly took you boys a long time."

"Yes, it certainly did."

Catherine came rushing back in. She sounded so excited.

"Come see; come and see! As soon as we got to the barn, she lay down and pushed out the most beautiful little foal. Oh, it was fast, and Iron Crow says it's a filly. She's a little chestnut and white thing. So tiny. Come see!"

Zane was laughing. He and his mother followed Catherine out to the barn.

"Who does this remind you of?" Iron Crow asked when Zane and Maggie peered over the stall door.

Iron Crow was rubbing the foal and talking softly to the mare in his native tongue. The foal had already tried to stand, and Iron Crow steadied her as she tried again.

"Spitting image of White Cloud." Zane was grinning from ear to ear.

"Even has his one red ear."

"Sure does."

"Well, what do you think, Catherine? Any special name for this little girl?" Iron Crow asked.

"Oh, I don't know. I've never named a horse before. Let me think. I know—what about White Cloud's Image? Will that work since she looks like your old pony, Zane?"

"I think it will work fine," Iron Crow said as he looked at his son with his sideways grin. Catherine giggled.

"I think that's a perfect name for her," Maggie said. "It's sweet. We can call her Image. This is going to be a good day to remember always."

~~~~

It was a difficult day as Catherine and Zane said goodbye to his parents. They didn't want to let go of him, and he didn't want to let go of them. Catherine had trouble saying goodbye as well.

Maggie held Catherine close and whispered something in her ear. The words flowed in a familiar way and sent chills down Catherine's spine, even though she didn't understand them.

"*Kitatama'sino*," Iron Crow said. "It means see you later. We don't like to say goodbye. There are no goodbyes in our language. We know we will always exist, no matter in what form. Here, there, over there. We can be shapeshifters or we can simply be."

"Stop it old fool," Maggie said, as she tucked her arm in his. "I know we will see you sooner than they think, won't we, Catherine? And, Iron Crow and I will be waiting right here," she said as she winked.

EPILOGUE

PARKER IRON CROW
AND MAGGIE WHITE CALF

AND

ZANE WHEELER
AND CATHERINE DELONG

REQUEST THE PRESENCE OF
YOUR COMPANY
TO CELEBRATE THEIR WEDDINGS

ON SATURDAY, JUNE 25, 2022
7:00 PM until . . .
AT THE WHEELER RANCH
dinner and shindig to follow

RSVP
P. O. Box *****, Choteau, MT 59422

www.ingramcontent.com/pod-product-compliance
Lightning Source LLC
Chambersburg PA
CBHW070543010526
44118CB00012B/1207